A CANADIAN'S GUIDE TO MONEY-SMART LIVING

KELLEY KEEHN

CA Chartered Accountants of Canada

Published by the Canadian Institute of Chartered Accountants

Disclaimer: Financial rates and regulations are constantly changing, so readers are advised to seek the advice of a financial professional to ensure that suggested strategies in this book are appropriate to their individual circumstances. All rates and calculations are current to October 19, 2012.

The CICA and the author do not accept any responsibility or liability that might occur directly or indirectly as a consequence of the use, application or reliance on this material.

Library and Archives Canada Cataloguing in Publication

Keehn, Kelley, date
A Canadian guide to money-smart living / Kelley Keehn.

Issued also in electronic format.
ISBN 978-1-55385-709-9

1. Finance, Personal--Canada. I. Canadian Institute of Chartered Accountants II. Title.

HG179.K423 2012 332.02400971 C2012-906198-0

Library and Archives Canada Cataloguing in Publication

Keehn, Kelley, date
A Canadian guide to money-smart living [electronic resource]
/ Kelley Keehn.

Electronic monograph in EPUB format.
Issued also in print format.
ISBN 978-1-55385-710-5

1. Finance, Personal--Canada. I. Canadian Institute of Chartered Accountants II. Title.

HG179.K423 2012 332.02400971 C2012-906199-9

The Canadian Institute of Chartered Accountants
277 Wellington Street West
Toronto ON M5V 3H2

Printed and bound in Canada

Table of Contents

Introduction 1

Chapter 1—Money 101 3

The Concept of Money is Changing 4
- Lifetime Earnings Really Add Up 5
- Why? Why? Why? 5

Take Control of Your Money 5
- Make the Effort 6

Life is Not Elsewhere 7
- Positive Decisions Are Empowering 7
  1. I Can Do This 7
  2. Spend Less Than You Earn 7
  3. Pay Yourself First 7

Prioritize 8
- Don't Let Them Trick you With Numbers 8

Top Five Excuses for Not Getting Started 9
  1. I don't have time 9
  2. I'm not smart enough 9
  3. My spouse will look after me 10
  4. I will be taken care of in my retirement by the government, my company pension, a lottery win, an inheritance, etc. 10
  5. It's too late for me to change 11
- Banish Negative Thoughts 11
  1. Shame 12
  2. Guilt 12
  3. Embarrassment 12
- Change Old Habits 12

Chapter 2—The Plan 15

What Do Apples and Sit-Ups Have to Do With Wealth? 16

A Comfortable Life is the Goal 17

Everyone Needs a Plan 18

Pay Yourself First 18

Save a Percentage of Your Gross Income 19

Pay Your Monthly Fixed Costs 19

The Budget Diet 20

The Budget Diet Step 1: Track Your Spending 21

The Budget Diet Step 2: Categorize Your Spending 21

The Budget Diet Step 3: Crunch the Numbers 22

The Budget Diet Step 4: Trim the Fat 22

Raising Questions 23

Getting Started: The Most Important Step 23

Categorize Your Spending Worksheet 25

Chapter 3—Simplify Your Life: Manage and Declutter 27

Keeping Good Records Helps You Achieve Financial Success 28

Getting and Staying Organized 29

Step 1: Start a Filing System 29

Step 2: Monitor Your Electronic and Paper Mail 29

Step 3: Contact Information 31

Two Distinct Types of Records That Must Be Kept 32

Permanent Records 32

Temporary Long-Term Records 33

Temporary Short-Term Records 33

Records You Should Destroy 33

Chapter 4—Important Financial Conversations 39

Talking with Your Spouse or Partner 40

The Six-Step Conversation 41

Step 1: What Are Our Goals? 41

Step 2: Needs and Wants List 42

Step 3: Where Are We Now? 43

Step 4: How Are We Going To Get To Our Goals? 43

Step 5: Make Changes 43

Step 6: Take Action and Get Help 43

Talking with Your Kids 44

Learn While You Teach 44

Talking with Your Parents 45

Talking with the Professionals 46

Important Issues to Discuss with Your Financial Planner 46

With Ken Costello, President and CEO of the Canadian Institute of Financial Planners 46

Important Issues to Discuss with Your Lawyer 47

With Yolanda Van Wachem of McLennan Ross LLP 47

Important Issues to Discuss with Your Life Insurance Agent 48

With Greg Pollock, President and CEO of Advocis, The Financial Advisors Association of Canada 48

Negotiating Outside the Family 51

Disputes 53

Chapter 5—Understanding Your Mortgage 55

My "Gut Reaction" Test 56

Terminology 57

Mortgage 57

Amortization 57

Term 57

Variable-Rate Mortgage 57

Fixed-Rate Mortgage 57

Your Biggest Expense 58

Mortgage Payments 58
Canadian Home Ownership 59
Paying Down the Mortgage 59

Preparing to Buy 60

Insurance 61
Title Insurance 61
Homeowner's Insurance 62
Mortgage (Life) Insurance 63
CMHC Mortgage Insurance 63

How to Buy a House 64
What Can They Afford? 67

Using Your RRSP for a Down Payment 68

Contribute to an RRSP or Pay Down the Mortgage? 69

Chapter 6—Managing Your Cash, Credit Cards and Other Debt 71

Cash 72
Keep Some Cash in Your House 72

Household Debt 73
Rising Consumer Debt 73
Just Managing Your Debt is Not Enough 73

Credit Cards 74
Always Carry a "Major" Credit Card 74
The Dangers of Department Store Cards 74
Just Applying for Credit Can Hurt Your Credit Score 74
How Many Credit Cards Should You Have? 75
Are Rewards Cards Worth the Hype? 75
Pros and Cons of Rewards Cards 75
Should You Worry about Fraud and Theft? 76
Lost or Stolen Cards 77
Credit Card Protection 77

Debit Cards 78
The Cost of Using Debit Cards 78

Emailing Money 79

Other Debt 79
Loans 79
Line of Credit 79
Consolidation Loan 80
Leasing 80

Dangers of Consumer Debt 81

Get Some Credit Even When You Don't Need It 82

Chapter 7—The Importance of a Good Credit Score 85

Why Credit is Important 86

Get to Know Your Banker 86

Check Your Credit Report Regularly 87
How to Get a Copy of Your Report 88
By Mail 88
Online Instantly 88

Understanding Your Score 89
What Does Your Score Mean For Your Credit Rating? 90
What Information is on Your Report? 90

Inquiries 93
Hard Inquiries 93
Soft Inquiries 94

How to Keep Your Credit Score Healthy 94

Some Important Credit Don'ts 98

Due Date vs. Statement Date 99

Supplementary Cards 100

Protect Your Identity 101

Dos and Don'ts to Help Protect Yourself 101
Conversation with Laurie Campbell (CEO, Credit Canada Debt Solutions) 103

Chapter 8—Investments for Today and for Your Future 107

Investing 101 108

Cash and Cash Equivalents 108
Savings Accounts 108
Term Deposits 109

Fixed Income 109
Guaranteed Investment Certificates (GICs) 109
Bonds 110
Bond Prices 111

Equity 111
Types of Shares 112
Preferred 112
Common 112
Dividend Reinvestment Plans [DRIPs] 112

Portfolio Management 113
Asset Allocation 113

Mutual Funds 114
Money Market Funds 114
Bond Funds 114
Equity Funds 115
Balanced Funds 115
Advantages of Mutual Funds 115
Disadvantages of Mutual Funds 115
High Cost 116
Poor Performance 117
Index Funds and Exchange Traded Funds 117
Index Funds 118
ETFs 118

Chapter 9—Tax Shelters to Help You Save Money and Defer Taxes 121

What is a Tax Shelter? 122

RRSPs 124
- Tax-Deferral 125
- Making Contributions 125
- Withdrawals 127
  - Lifelong Learning Plan 127
  - Home Buyers' Plan 127
- Filing Your Income Taxes 127
- When Not to Invest in an RRSP 128
- RRSP vs. Non-RRSP Savings 128
  - Inside a Tax Shelter or Outside? 128

RRIFs 129
- Converting Your RRSP into a RRIF 130
  - Using Age to Your Advantage 131
  - Resheltering Can Save Taxes 131
  - Withdrawals Can Affect Your OAS 131

RESPs 131
- Family RESPs 132
- Multiple Plans 132
- Canada Education Savings Grant 133
- Canada Learning Bond 133

TFSAs 133
- Contributions in After-Tax Dollars 134
- TFSA or RRSP? 134
  - Advantages of RRSPs 134
  - Advantages of TFSAs 135

RDSPs 135

The Garages 138

Chapter 10—It's Never Too Late to Start Being Money Smart! 143

1. Start by Saving More 144

Pay Yourself First 144

2. Start Spending Less 145

Put Yourself on the "30-Day Budget Diet" 145

3. Start Managing Your Cash, Credit Cards and Other Debt 145

Try to Say "No" to More Debt! 146

Ready, Set, Go! 147

Resources 149

Acknowledgements 155

About the Author 157

Introduction

The genesis of this project came about from a presentation I gave to the Institute of Chartered Accountants of Alberta in Calgary in 2011. During the Q&A section of my talk, there were a number of interesting comments and conversations from the audience. What struck me most during the question period was the genuine concern that CAs have for the financial education of their clients and their family members as well as for the Canadian public as a whole.

One older CA lamented about his frustration that our public school systems have incorporated sex education from an early age right up to teenage years, yet not one course is dedicated to financial literacy for our youth. He also noted, interestingly, that even though I write books and make a wide variety of media appearances via television, radio, newspapers and more, that I probably wasn't reaching our youth in furthering my mission to make Canadians **feel good about money**. He commented that his grandchildren and their friends don't get their news from traditional sources now, they receive most of their information online from Facebook, YouTube and more. So, if we're not reaching them during their years of education and their parents likely also don't have a firm financial foundation, how will financial literacy ever change in Canada?

I was fortunate to chat with Katie Starratt after that presentation who informed me of the ICAA's provincial initiatives for financial literacy in Alberta. She later introduced me to Cairine Wilson, Vice-President of Member Services with the Canadian Institute of Chartered Accountants (CICA), who equally shared the passion of CAs across Canada to educate our nation. From my years in the financial industry, I have always known how widely respected the CA profession is (I like to refer to them as the surgeons of the financial industry), but I was thrilled to learn how many volunteer hours (during their own extremely busy tax season) many CAs across the country dedicate to the public by volunteering their time to prepare tax returns for low income individuals free of charge, many of whom might never be able to reciprocate with payment or become a future client. The CAs do it because they care and want to make a difference.

When Cairine explained that the CICA was ready to be the first national organization to roll out a financial literacy education program and that there were CAs ready to volunteer their time to provide free educational sessions to individuals and businesses, I was thrilled to participate. This book is the companion to their much-needed program.

Kelley Keehn

August 2012

CHAPTER 1

MONEY 101

Money isn't everything...
but it ranks right up there with oxygen.

—Rita Davenport

Money 101

When I think back to my own schooling, by the end of high school none of my teachers had talked about money management, i.e., saving, investing, budgeting, mortgages and loans, having a great credit score and the other day-to-day issues of managing money. The accounting and economics courses were very interesting, but they were too abstract and didn't deal with the here and now. During my whole public school education, the only money-management lesson I ever got was from my grade eight teacher, who warned us never to use our credit cards unless we could afford to pay for the purchase in cash. I remember thinking: "If you can afford to buy something with cash, why would you ever need a credit card? Don't people use credit cards because they want things they really can't afford?"

The Concept of Money is Changing

Most of what I learned about money management in those days came from my mother and her impeccable money management skills. Her favourite expression was: "Money doesn't grow on trees." Even though she was a single parent raising three children within very modest means, my mother almost always paid with cash, reconciled her bank statements each month and negotiated a better price whenever possible. My fear today is how nebulous "money" or currency has become. I think if my mother were a parent today, she might declare to me, "Money doesn't grow in plastic." Many kids today don't fully grasp where money comes from as they see their parents hand clerks a piece of plastic and then punch a few numbers on a PIN pad. As I write this, the Canadian government recently announced that they're stopping the production of pennies as the cost is too high. I fear the greater cost is a cashless society which no longer comprehends the concept of money when spending. On the rare occasions when my mother used her credit card, she would stop and give me the stern warning: "If you must buy something on credit, make sure you pay it off, in full, every month". Prudent advice, and she always paid off the purchase by the due date. Needless to say, my mother had perfect credit.

Lifetime Earnings Really Add Up

As I grew older I came to realize that my mother and my grade eight teacher were very wise. I recognized how much we need to learn at a very early age about handling our own money. The reason is simple: a lot of money is going to pass through your hands over your earning lifetime. No matter what you do for a living, you're going to earn a lot and, since you are also going to spend a lot, understanding how money works will be essential to your personal success and happiness. As of January 2012, Canadians had an average annual salary of about $46,000, according to Statistics Canada. As an example, let's suppose that is the average salary for 40 years of working life. At that rate, $1,840,000 (almost $2 million!) will pass through your hands. If you have a two-income household, this amount would approximately double to $3,680,000. If you earn more than the average Canadian, you will see even more than that will come into your bank account over your working life.

Why? Why? Why?

So, if we earn so much money, why are so many Canadians living from pay cheque to pay cheque? Why are so many Canadians burdened with excessive amounts of consumer debt? And why are we not better off when it comes to retirement? The answer lies in how we manage our money while we're earning it. How do we balance saving, spending, wants, needs, cash flow, debt and the many other factors that result in the financial expression of who we think ourselves to be or want to be?

You're going to earn a lot in your lifetime and, since you are also going to spend a lot, understanding how money works will be essential to your personal success and happiness.

Take Control of Your Money

Being good with money is not a mystery. It's within the reach of everyone who is willing to learn and wants to take control of their present and future finances. The question is: What do you need to know? You will be relieved to learn you do not need to know the mathematics of hedge-fund trading or how to survive in the futures market. All you really need to know is how to manage *your own* money. This knowledge can be mastered by anyone willing to learn a few basic but *very* important concepts and willing to set up the rules to win. Let me liken the goal of a healthy financial life to that of a healthy physical life. We can visualize the latter and the basic principles are logical to us all. We know that fad diets don't work (or not for long) and simple solutions, such as eating less and building up our muscles through exercise, take time. The same is true with finance, although the solutions might seem less obvious and be more frustrating. But a little patience with building your "money muscles" and a willingness to not overlook simple strategies will ensure your long-term success.

When I was in my twenties, I worked for one of Canada's international banks. My job was to provide advice and invest money for high-net-worth individuals. You may be surprised to learn that many of my multi-millionaire customers were average wage earners with very average incomes. Many were investors of modest means who managed to invest a portion of their salaries regularly enough to have accumulated impressive portfolios. What these people realized was that successful management of their own financial affairs was not a secret known only to those who work on Bay Street.

Make the Effort

The means of understanding money management is within your hands. A client of mine decided he wanted to understand jazz. So he went online and researched a variety of Internet resources, watched YouTube, downloaded free books from the library and read the basics about the history of jazz and the great musicians, bought many tracks on iTunes and within about six months was very comfortable in the world of jazz. He was no expert, but he could now appreciate what he was listening to. Becoming knowledgeable about jazz was always within his grasp. He just had to make the effort to learn.

Learning about financial management is much like my client's experience learning about jazz. You have the ability to become comfortable managing your own finances. You too can effortlessly learn about your finances without ever leaving your home! Plus, immersion can be the best source of learning. My friend could attend jazz festivals, start learning the sax or go to a groovy club. You could equally join one of the many online communities or start a money group or investment club.

Life is Not Elsewhere

Sadly, there are too many people who go through their lives in a state of permanent discontent, thinking "life is elsewhere". If only I had more money, if only I were better looking, if only my parents had been rich, if only I had other friends, etc. If only they could realize that they have all the means of achieving their own happiness right in their hands at any given moment, they could do something to bring about their own happiness. All they need to do is to summon up the willpower to make a few difficult but important decisions.

Positive Decisions Are Empowering

Once a positive decision has been made, it's amazing how much strength a person can find within themselves to carry it through. Three simple concepts will get you started:

1. I Can Do This

You can learn enough about financial management to manage your own money for your lifetime so you can live well and retire comfortably. With this Guide, you'll also be empowered to know how to interview financial professionals along the way. Part of living well is feeling secure about your money. Knowing your savings are growing and that you are paying off your mortgage allows you to sleep at night. You also know that if the worst happens and you're one of the unlucky ones to be downsized or divorced, you can weather the storm.

2. Spend Less Than You Earn

This sounds like a cliché and it is. But clichés carry more than a kernel of truth. The big kernel here is that money spent is money *not* saved. And if you love spending, consider spending a percentage on a very important aspect of your life: You! Which leads us to the next concept.

3. Pay Yourself First

Pay yourself first! Save before you spend.

The third decision is so important it's worth repeating: ***Pay yourself first***. Save before you spend. Do not look upon savings as something left over after you've spent everything else. Save first, live and budget with the net amount. Remember when we looked at what an individual or couple is likely to earn in their lifetime? If you saved just 10%, not factoring in investment growth, you'd have $184,000 (or $368,000 for a couple) by just skimming a little off the top. Plus, with some investment acumen, that number would be significantly higher (at 7% growth, for example, your money would double every 10 years). I can assure you that even if you put that 10% under your mattress (not a good idea), you'd still have more than the average Canadian at retirement.

Prioritize

The sad truth is that so many individuals will spend more time planning a vacation than they will spend looking at their financial or retirement needs. Too many of us end up doing in real life what Mark Twain once said in jest: "Never put off till tomorrow what you can do the day after tomorrow."

Saving is not something to be done tomorrow. It starts today. Here and now. You have both the means and the time to be financially successful. Just look at how many hours you have each year to work on your financial plans. Let's start with the 8,760 hours we have at our disposal every year. If you subtract the 2,000 hours you spend working 40 hours a week (50 weeks a year) and the 2,920 hours spent sleeping 8 hours every night, you are left with 3,840 hours or 43.8% of your life as free time. That's almost half a year in which to accomplish something important.

In the early, low-income-earning years, we promise ourselves that when we earn more, we'll save. Then we procrastinate. The noteworthy point is that if we can't save a percentage of our income when it's low, we certainly won't when it's higher. If good saving habits aren't formed early on, we will usually find ways to increase our wants (or what we justify as "needs") and therefore increase our expenses. You can start forming those great saving habits now!

Don't Let Them Trick you With Numbers

So, if it's so simple, why don't we just do it? Why do we value so many other things and activities more than taking care of our money? Why do we not take ourselves more seriously and be more self-disciplined? Because our short-term demands always seem to get the best of us.

The few dollars you spend on muffins, eating out, or other expenditures that you're not tracking every day, might not seem like much at the time but mount up over the weeks and months and years. Retailers love to hook us in with "it's only $5 a day or $35 a week". They know most of us won't bother to add that up over a year and induce us to spend more by presenting smaller amounts. What they don't want you to do is add up the numbers. That $5-a-day indulgence becomes a $35-a-week habit and, before you know it, you've spent $1,820 per year of after-tax dollars! That's the cost of a trip each year (or several staycations) by simply not being aware of your daily spending. The bottom line is that we can't deceive ourselves in the short term and ignore our small expenditures.

Top Five Excuses for Not Getting Started

1. I don't have time

Yes, you do! Remember, you have 3,840 hours a year of free time. Getting up 10 minutes earlier (ideally, before the kids) adds five extra hours a month of available time! You have to take care of your money if you want it to take care of you. Use the time to:

- Check your online bank accounts.
- Check rates on mortgages, GICs, term deposits, etc., on bank websites as there may be deals.
- Read about mutual funds.
- Add up your family's monthly spending. Are the amounts less than the family income? If not, why not?
- Make time to teach your children about money. They imitate your behaviour in all aspects of life, including money.

2. I'm not smart enough

Yes, you are! Remember, this is not difficult. You just have to care enough to get some information!

- **Don't be intimidated.** Think about talking to your financial advisor or banker as you would your doctor. Do some research and ask some questions. You wouldn't hesitate to ask your doctor about your health, so why hesitate to discuss anything and everything about your money with the bank?

- **Get curious.** You don't need to know everything. Just care enough to start! Begin a list of questions to ask your banker or financial planner (see **Chapter 4: Important Financial Conversations**).
- **Fraud.** Many victims of fraud get taken because they do not know what questions to ask that would raise suspicions. Victims of fraud all have one thing in common; they failed to pay attention to details. We're going to look at how to protect your identity in **Chapter 7: The Importance of a Good Credit Score**.
- **Fear.** Trusted professionals can guide you through uncertain times and should help to keep you grounded so your expectations are reasonable.

3. My spouse will look after me

This may not necessarily be true. It is safer if you don't rely on others (and that includes your spouse). No one will care more about your finances than you do. Even if you are dependent on your spouse now, you still need to be aware of your income, debts and investments.

- Since 40% of all marriages in Canada end in divorce, there is a possibility you may need to rely on your own earning and saving power at some point in your life.
- Accidents happen. A person can be widowed or forced to become the breadwinner when a spouse is incapacitated. Substantial money management skills will be needed if you suddenly become a single parent.

4. I will be taken care of in my retirement by the government, my company pension, a lottery win, an inheritance, etc.

These are all bad ideas!

- The Old Age Security (OAS) the government provides is not sufficient to maintain a middle-class lifestyle. If you rely on government support, you will be living at or below the poverty level. At $510.21 per month, the OAS amounts to only $6,123 per year per person (in 2012). While Canada has no official "poverty line", the Low Income Cut Off of Statistics Canada for 2012 considers a person to be in poverty if they are earning less than $18,759 per year. The government doesn't want you to rely on public funding for your retirement; that's why it created the Registered Retirement Savings Plan (RRSP) and Tax-Free Savings Accounts (TFSAs) to help you save for retirement.

- Companies go bankrupt, go out of business, are sold or merged with other companies that want to reduce the cost of pension plans. Remember what happened to the jobs, pensions and stock options of employees who relied on employers such as Enron and Nortel?
- Having a lottery win as part of your financial plan is absurd. The chance of winning the lottery is approximately 1 in 14 million.
- Inheritances have a habit of not being as big or coming as soon as you expected. With so many people living longer, there is a substantial risk they will run down their capital significantly before they die and you may receive little or nothing.

5. It's too late for me to change

Not true! It's never too late to take control of your money.

- Many people think that because they're getting close to retirement and don't have any substantial savings there's no hope and therefore no point in starting so late. Actually, many people don't start saving until this time in their lives because of mortgages and their children's education. Our most expensive years are usually those leading up to mid-life. As a result, the years from your late 40s and early 50s and beyond can be the easiest years for saving. The absence of mortgage and education costs plus high income levels means you can still catch up! Many of my past clients didn't really start to save aggressively until their 50s and older!

It's never too late to take control of your money.

Banish Negative Thoughts

When it comes to managing your money (or lack thereof) in your family, the top excuses for putting things off can be a host of uncomfortable emotions. The following three emotions are holding individuals back from confidently taking charge. Defining what you're feeling is a great first step in order to tame the "enemy" and move forward. Think about the following emotions in the context of your own financial situation:

1. Shame

A period of hard times because of unemployment or divorce, poverty in one's childhood and other factors can make a person ashamed of their financial health. Just remember you deserve the best possible life despite these setbacks.

2. Guilt

Have you ever made a purchase that you felt terrible about later or even hidden from your family? Did you and your spouse take a vacation that wasn't enjoyable because you couldn't stop worrying about how you were going to pay for it? If you feel guilty about your spending, it's probably because you bought a "want" item and not a "need" item. When you knowingly set money aside and save up for these products and services, not only does the guilt disappear, your level of enjoyment and satisfaction dramatically increases as well.

3. Embarrassment

Not everyone feels bad about their financial circumstances, but they probably feel they should know and do more. In an area as vast as your financial life, even the brightest professionals don't know everything about accounting, investing, banking, budgeting and more. They're not embarrassed, so why should you be?

Change Old Habits

If we applied some decisiveness to our financial affairs, would we soon develop wealth-building habits? What if we saved a portion of every pay cheque by having a portion taken off the top automatically every payday and saved? What if we had a family financial meeting on the first of the month, no matter what? What if we pre-arranged an annual meeting with our banker to discuss paying down our debts, and with our financial planners to figure out how to save more? Not some appointment we know we *should* set one day but never do, but an appointment set in advance, carved in stone and taken out of our daily to-do list.

More of our day is spent acting automatically than is spent acting as a result of conscious decisions, i.e., much of what we do every day is simply a repeat of what we did the day before. We get up, shower, go to work, come home, eat supper and go to bed. What's already set out as a pattern is easier to complete. So why not remove the need for making a lot of future decisions by setting up savings and other financial management routines that we do automatically? If you add these habits to your regular routine, before long it will be just as automatic as taking that morning shower.

Easy Action Steps

1. **Pick one week to get up just five minutes earlier and use the time to research holiday destinations before you choose one, or get curious about your finances over your morning cup of coffee.**

2. **List your financial emotions. They don't need to rule you—you can tame them by naming them!**

3. **Start your journey on your own bank's website. They'll have lots of calculators and articles to get you started!**

CHAPTER 2

THE PLAN

Every day is a bank account, and time
is our currency. No one is rich,
no one is poor, we've got 24 hours each.

—Christopher Rice

The Plan

You may have heard of the concept of the *Latte Factor*®. The author, David Bach, introduced the concept in his book, *The Automatic Millionaire*. It essentially makes the case for giving up your daily, expensive latte and allocating those dollars to your retirement. While I think it may be a brilliant idea to give up your daily coffee habit and save that money for retirement, I have to admit—it's not for me. Handling your money well is not just about awareness; it's also about choice. It's all very well to talk about giving up your lattes and retiring on the money you'll save, but who wants to give up something they really love? *Forever!* Surely, the reason for having more money is to enjoy it and the freedom it provides? The point is: if the sacrifice is too great, we won't stick with a plan over the long term. This is where choice really comes into play; when it comes to money management, you get to choose what's most important to you. I choose not to give up my daily latte habit, but I might sacrifice something of less importance to me to achieve the same goal.

This chapter looks at ways to stretch your money without suffering unduly.

What Do Apples and Sit-Ups Have to Do With Wealth?

It's been said that we're only concerned about our health and wealth to the extent that we don't have them. This is very true. When you recover from the flu, you're ready to do somersaults the first day you're back to normal or, if you sprain your ankle and it finally heals, you feel like a new person capable of running a marathon. But before you became ill or injured, you didn't think about how good it felt *not* to be sick or hurt.

Good physical and financial health have a lot in common. In theory, it should be easy to keep healthy by shedding some excess weight or remaining thin. Just two simple principles apply: *eat less and exercise more*. Eat an apple instead of a muffin when you need a snack. Do some sit-ups on the living room floor while you're watching TV. Doing a little bit at a time and doing it regularly can do a lot for your fitness.

Being financially healthy requires the same discipline. You probably wouldn't expect to live a long, healthy life if you smoked, took drugs, drank too much, ate too much and never exercised. The same principles apply to your financial health. If you overspend on a flashy car or buy a bigger house than you can carry if mortgage rates increase, you may be gambling with your financial health. So, if we all know we should work out to keep fit and save money to be financially secure, why don't we do that? Why do we value so many other things over our physical and financial health—both now and for the future? The answer is very simple: short-term demands overrule long-term goals. Whether it's $1 spent, or a chocolate bar eaten each day, they all add up. We can cheat in the short term, but time is a masterful compounder.

A Comfortable Life is the Goal

After years of talking to people about their personal finances, one message comes through loud and clear: what most people want is not a life of fabulous wealth, but one in which they can pursue the things they love because they have the financial means to do so, and can do it worry free. Having a relaxed annual vacation in your favourite place shouldn't seem too much to expect. But, just as good health doesn't come without a modicum of sacrifice, neither does financial security. I'm sure you will agree that both goals are well worth the effort.

A comfortable lifestyle and a worry-free retirement are achievable only if you are willing to exercise the self-discipline required to do this the moment your earned income hits your bank account. I'm not talking about applying some complex budget plan to your pay cheque that requires you to watch every penny in order to squeeze out something at the end of the month to be put away and called "savings". I'm talking about setting aside something from every pay cheque *before* you do your spending. The truth is that it is almost impossible not to indulge ourselves if we have the money in hand. The "trick" is to never see the savings portion in the first place: out of sight, out of mind.

Good physical and financial health have a lot in common

And that trick is the essential key. We know from new research that will power is exhaustible. If I want to stick to a weight loss goal, it's a great deal easier if I don't have to resist temptation. If my husband brings home my favourite dessert, I now have to use my will power to forgo the tasty treat. However, if he simply doesn't bring it home at all, I don't have to give anything up. So make sure your savings are deducted before the funds ever hit your account.

Everyone Needs a Plan

Let's start at the beginning: your earnings. Unless you win the lottery or inherit from a long line of thrifty ancestors, your only source of funds will be your earnings. Once you get paid, you can either save or spend. Out of your earnings must come not only the money to be saved and invested to provide income many years down the road, but also money to be spent for day-to-day living.

Conventional budgeting asks you to pay all your bills first, then save whatever is left over: saving becomes optional, but it should be mandatory. This rarely works because it's too easy to ignore the savings part of the budget. When saving comes last, it often doesn't happen at all.

In fact, conventional budgeting usually works about as well as a fad diet. Maybe for a month or two we can keep track of our income and outgoings but, after that, everything seems to slip back into the same bad old routine.

Putting your own plan in place is really very simple; carrying it out is even easier. Just follow these three basic steps:

1. **Pay Yourself First**
2. **Pay Your Monthly Fixed Costs**
3. **Follow the Budget Diet**

Pay Yourself First

The key decision behind the success of any money management plan is always, always, always to ***pay yourself first*** before you even think about paying for your monthly expenditures.

"But I can't afford that! It already takes all the money I earn just to make ends meet!" Money should be like time, we should make time for what's truly important. Since only about 32% of the Canadian labour force has a company pension plan, the chances are that you do not have a company plan. As a result, it is going to be your responsibility to save for your own retirement. Not only is paying yourself first essential to your long-term financial planning, asking you to take money off the top is asking you to do nothing more than those friends in pension plans are already doing every pay day: they authorize their employer to deduct money from their pay and put it in a pension fund to provide an income for retirement.

These employees apply their budget plan to their *net* income. In fact, you too are already doing this to some extent. Your employer deducts your Canada Pension Plan contribution before depositing your pay into your bank account. Money is taken right off the top to create your Canada Pension and you don't miss it because you don't see it. Nevertheless, it is doing something very important for you; it's going to build a fund for your future.

Save a Percentage of Your Gross Income

Some people use the 10% factor (which means that 10% of their gross income is the magic number for savings). If that amount works for you, and you are diligent about sustaining this—great. Or, you might ask a friend with an income similar to yours and who has a company pension plan what percentage of their gross income is deducted right off the top of their pay for their pension plan. Arrange to put a similar amount aside for yourself every month and treat that amount as a fixed cost. Start by using your bank's pre-authorized transfer service to take money out of every pay and put into a special savings account. We'll look at the best strategies for maximizing your savings in **Chapter 8: Investments**.

Save at least 10% of your gross income, or more, if possible.

Pay Your Monthly Fixed Costs

After paying yourself first by setting aside savings, the remainder of your earnings is available for:

1. paying your rent/mortgage and other monthly bills, and
2. spending on yourself and your family.

Your monthly bills are a fixed cost that must be paid every month without any decisions having to be made. Some, such as your rent/mortgage and insurance premiums, are the same each month. Others, like water, electricity, telephone, etc., are paid monthly or every other month. These amounts may vary slightly but they still have to be paid. If you're paying online, make sure you pay the bill a few days before the due date in order for the payment to clear and reach the merchant by the due date. Do not leave it until the due date; you will almost certainly be charged a late fee if you do.

The money left over after you have paid your mandatory monthly bills is the money you can actually think about and budget. These are the amounts you can choose to spend or not to spend.

The Budget Diet

I'm often asked how to set and stick to a budget. I always reply with the same answer: *I hate budgets because they rarely work*. If you were eating 2,500 calories a day and a diet forced you to eat only 1,500 calories, you'd likely never last. Sure, the results would be there, but giving up too much too soon ensures failure in the long term.

So why not focus your fiscal thinking on how to make the most of the money available for you and your family to enjoy? The purpose of this kind of thinking is to get rid of the waste that sees your discretionary money just dribble away in unfocused spending. Tracking your spending will reveal how much of your discretionary income might be misdirected away from maximum enjoyment. Just as we thoughtlessly consume empty calories by continuing to eat even when we're not really hungry, we can carelessly create financial waste. You might be surprised at how much.

To manage your money better, you'll need to start by counting your financial calories. The ***30-Day Budget Diet*** is an eye-opening exercise that's entertaining and can involve the entire family.

If you want to spend $450 a month enjoying restaurant meals, you can't waste money on small daily purchases like bottled water, coffee and lunches. I can't tell you to spend only $200 a month eating out and I can't tell you to slash your spending in certain areas if that's what gets you up in the morning or excited for the weekend. But I know with almost 100% certainty there are areas of your financial life where you will find waste.

The Budget Diet Step 1: Track Your Spending

For the next 30 days track what you and your family spend. And I mean every single dollar—not just the cash you spend, but every pre-authorized payment and every debit and credit transaction. This is essentially the same exercise recommended for people preparing to physically diet: for 30 days you write down everything you eat and measure the calories. At the end of the month the desire to cut back will be irresistible. But that's not the purpose of this exercise. I simply want you and your family to get a one-month snapshot of your normal spending patterns.

The Budget Diet Step 2: Categorize Your Spending

Now that you have collected data for a month, group your spending into categories such as:

- rent/mortgage
- insurance
- utilities
- loans
- car payments
- credit card payments
- gas
- car maintenance and more
- parking tickets
- late charges and penalty charges
- groceries
- eating out
- cable/satellite/Internet
- cell phones
- entertainment
- habits (good—gym membership—and bad—smoking, drinking, gambling)
- hobbies
- children's extra curriculum activities (trips, dues, sports fees and equipment)
- self-improvement

Some smartphones and tablets have an App for tracking and categorizing your spending or see the sample sheet at the end of this chapter and **www.financialdecisionsmatter.com** for an Excel file.

If you have some unique categories that contain regular expenditures, add them to the list. You want an honest snapshot of where the monthly dollars are going.

The Budget Diet Step 3: Crunch the Numbers

Numbers are your friend. You don't have to be good at math to "crunch" the numbers which you need to keep yourself from harmful overspending. For example, retailers work really hard to convince you to look only at the short term and not crunch the long-term numbers. It's only $3 a day to buy that new TV after all—less than the price of your favourite coffee. But, oops, you didn't notice that the interest rate on the balance is 29% which means you'll have paid three times the sticker price once you've finished with the financing for that $3-a-day TV. This is the kind of thing that should be revealed by a month of tracking expenses.

Take the monthly results and multiply them by 12. There's no room for judgment here—this is simply an eye-opener for you and your family as to what you're spending each year on certain categories.

The Budget Diet Step 4: Trim the Fat

Now that you know how your family allocates its money, take the list and talk together about how much real enjoyment you're all getting out of living like this. Places where you can cut back will probably leap off the page. I'm not asking you to cut out entire categories as many traditional budgets may ask you to do. I simply want awareness to drive you and your family. I don't know one person who's completed this exercise who hasn't been shocked by some category. I spend how much on *that*? And that adds up to *what* in a year and *how much* in 10 years??? A friend of mine did this exercise once and was stunned to find that he spent $350 a year on getting the daily paper delivered when he could read it online for free. That's the kind of awareness I was mentioning earlier.

With our calorie intake, we need to have a daily limit. The same is true for our financial calories.

If, after tracking and discussing the family spending pattern, you find out that entertainment is more important to your family than travel, so be it. If having a great TV and cable package creates and strengthens family time and saves money on going out to the movies, that's wonderful. But remember—just as with our actual calories, we need to have a daily limit. The same is true for our financial calories.

Raising Questions

Your financial life doesn't have to be just about spending less, cutting back and sacrifice. It can also be about more—more income that is! As you get creative in trimming the financial fat, spend at least an equal amount of time brainstorming income-generating ideas. Is there a part-time business that you've always wanted to start? Items in the house or garage that might fetch enough for a small trip by selling them on eBay, Kijiji or Craigslist? Maybe you could sell your baked goods or crafts at a farmers' market? What about helping your kids sell their old toys and electronics? Or perhaps your teenager could teach computer courses to other kids or maybe even in seniors' homes? The ideas are endless. You don't need to necessarily take on a second job. Get creative within your social circle as well. What do they need or want? Perhaps you love cooking or cleaning and have friends who despise both and would gladly pay for your help? And don't forget about good old-fashioned barter. Do your friends have items or provide services that you could trade for? Perhaps you could start a Facebook page with your friends dedicated to swapping products and services with each other.

Getting Started: The Most Important Step

The ideal moment to start your financial plan is right now. There will never be a better time. Remember what I said in **Chapter 1**: Life is not elsewhere or tomorrow; it is here and now. You have the means in your hands today to take action for yourself. Yes, interest rates are historically low and the stock market is constantly volatile. Nevertheless, unless you believe no government or corporation will ever have to borrow money again and no company will ever sell more of its products and services and make profits, there will be growth opportunities in the future for which you can prepare by saving today. What's the alternative? To consume all your income and *not* save? Absolutely not! You're worth it—start saving for you!

Easy Action Steps

1. Remember that the principles of health and wealth are closely connected. A chocolate bar, an apple or a dollar a day adds up. Contact your bank and set up a savings plan. Even if you start with just $25 or $50 a month, once you see your account grow, the habit will become effortless.

2. Set a date to start the Budget Diet. The 1st of the month is a perfect time to start.

3. Brainstorm 5 to 10 ideas for earning more income with family and friends and then choose one or two to try.

Categorize Your Spending Worksheet*

Spending Categories

	$
rent/mortgage	
insurance	
utilities	
loans	
car payments	
credit card payments	
gas	
car maintenance and more	
parking tickets	
late charges and penalty charges	
groceries	
eating out	
cable/satellite/Internet	
cell phones	
entertainment	
habits (good and bad – smoking, drinking, gambling)	
hobbies	
gym memberships	
children's extra curriculum (trips, dues, sports fees and equipment)	
self-improvement	

*See **www.financialdecisionsmatter.com** for a Word file.

CHAPTER 3

SIMPLIFY YOUR LIFE: MANAGE AND DECLUTTER

I love money. I love everything about it.
I bought some pretty good stuff. Got me
a $300 pair of socks. Got a fur sink.
An electric dog polisher. A gasoline powered
turtleneck sweater. And, of course,
I bought some dumb stuff, too.

—Steve Martin

Simplify Your Life: Manage and Declutter

We all have them and can't get rid of them. They take far more of our time than we think they should, but we can't do without them. They can be frustrating and can even weigh us down. They are one of life's burdens.

I'm talking about records, of course. Whether they're paper or electronic, we always seem to have too many of them, can't seem to find the ones we need, and our lives are cluttered with the ones we may never use.

This chapter will guide you through the maze of record-keeping to help you decide which documents you should have at your fingertips, which should be filed, which should be shredded, and which records must be kept for eternity (or at least your lifetime!).

Keeping Good Records Helps You Achieve Financial Success

You may be surprised to learn that your financial success depends on how well you take care of your financial and other important documents. It is essential to know where everything is, what you need to keep, what you can safely dispose of, and where you stand at all times. Information that cannot be found is worthless. A lost receipt could be a lost deductible business expense and a lost record could prove to be expensive because it is not available to substantiate a claim.

Records are evidence that something has happened: invoices come in and payments go out; paper trails are an inevitable outcome of normal day-to-day living. But it is important to distinguish between the records that need to be kept forever, those that need to be kept just for a few years, and those that can be disposed of as soon as they've been attended to. Many of the documents you need to keep concern your taxes: income taxes, property (household) taxes, capital gains taxes, or sales taxes for large purchases. If you're running a business from your home, you will also need to keep detailed records for the Canada Revenue Agency (CRA) in case you ever get audited.

Getting and Staying Organized

How do you and your family organize your records? Can you find your T4 slips at income tax time, or do you just throw important papers into an overflowing junk drawer?

Step 1: Start a Filing System

Think about what system would work best for your home or small office to keep all your documents in order. Designate a place in the house that would be convenient to keep your incoming mail, important documents and to pay your bills. This will probably be your computer desk. You should have a place (e.g., an accordion file folder, or maybe a small file cabinet) for keeping the paper copies of any monthly statements you may need for your tax filing at the end of the year, or for your long-term records.

You need a safety deposit box or home safe for wills and other important documents, such as your power of attorneys, deed to your home and more.

When it comes to paying bills, however, the Internet has provided us with the following paperless options:

1. a paper bill received in the mail but paid online through an account set up with your bank;
2. an electronic bill received online and paid online through an account set up with your bank.

Try paperless for paying bills: Consider getting a USB drive to back up your essential electronic documents twice a year (maybe your pictures too) and store it offsite in perhaps your safety deposit box.

You can keep the paper originals, of course. You can also copy the electronic version to an electronic folder on your computer or print off a copy.

Step 2: Monitor Your Electronic and Paper Mail

Make a master list of all of your bills, the dates they usually arrive and their payment due dates. This list should be kept in your designated workplace, preferably as an electronic master file on your computer. Check off your bills as they arrive (whether by mail or email). Missing mail may be the first sign of

Keep your list accessible in a safe place, such as your home safe or safety deposit box. Your executors and agents with power of attorney should know the location of these. However, be careful with this information because, although most banks provide protection against fraud, the banks and credit card companies might not reimburse you if they can prove you didn't keep your PINs secure and private.

Two Distinct Types of Records That Must Be Kept

Some records need to be kept just for short periods of time, others must be kept forever. Permanent records mark events that may need to be referred to years later. The temporary documents are evidence of day-to-day activities that show mainly how money is moving through your accounts, i.e., what is owed and what is paid and when.

(See the end of this chapter and **www.financialdecisionsmatter.com** for sample checklists.)

Permanent Records

Keep the following as permanent records:

- birth certificate
- marriage certificate
- will
- living will
- powers of attorney for property and personal care
- Social Insurance Number card
- health cards
- insurance policies for home and auto
- mortgage papers
- personal line of credit and other loan documents
- pre-planned funeral documents
- diplomas
- warranties for autos, appliances, TVs and electronic equipment.

Temporary Long-Term Records

Probably the most important temporary long-term documents you need to keep are the income and expense records you use to complete your income tax filing each year. The Canada Revenue Agency (CRA) requires records "to be kept for a minimum of six years from the end of the last tax year to which they relate". These records are important to support your expense claims in case of a CRA audit. Your records can be in either paper or electronic format, but keeping the originals is better. If you bank online and need bank statements, print off the page immediately. Banks do not keep this information available online forever and it can be quite expensive to ask the bank to search for old information.

Make sure you keep accurate records of:

- child care expenses
- charitable donations
- medical expenses
- spousal or child support payments
- RRSP contributions
- moving expenses, etc., and
- income tax returns.

If you own investments, trade confirmations and statements from your broker should also be kept so you can calculate your capital gains and losses.

Temporary Short-Term Records

Unless there is some kind of ongoing dispute, normal bills for utilities, credit cards and other household expenses that are not going to be used as deductions when filing income tax can probably be disposed of after six to twelve months.

Records You Should Destroy

Documents that are not related to your tax filings or are part of your permanent documents should usually be destroyed after one year. Automatic Teller Machine (ATM) slips and utility/phone bills, etc., just become clutter after a while.

Shred any documents with your name, address, and credit card, bank and any household account numbers, or other personal identifiers. Identity theft is always a risk!

- Consider going paperless by setting up electronic files.
- Read all credit card and bank statements, utility bills and other invoices carefully to ensure they're accurate and confirm that amounts charged are correct (better yet, keep track online), but you don't need to keep them for longer than six to twelve months.

Easy Action Steps

1. Get organized. Find a spot in your home for bill paying and filing documents.
2. At the start of each week, check all of your account balances, read through your purchases online to ensure they're correct and add due dates for bills to your online calendar.
3. See **www.financialdecisionsmatter.com** to print the checklists (also following this chapter) to help you manage and declutter your records.

Sample Monthly Payments Checklist*

Bill/Statement	Arrival due date	Arrived	Due date	Paid
Telephone				
Cell phone				
Cable/Internet				
Chequing account				
Savings account				
Visa				
MasterCard				
American Express				
Store credit card				
Gas				
Hydro				
Mortgage				
Insurance premium				
Property taxes				
Income tax notice of assessment				

*See **www.financialdecisionsmatter.com** for a Word file of this checklist.

Contact Information*

Document	Account number(s)	Location/Contact
Bank(s)		
Wills		
Living Will		
Powers of attorney		
Safety deposit box		
Safety deposit box key		
Doctor		
Health care provider		
Health Insurance number		
Social Insurance number		
Real estate documents		
Financial planner		
Investment advisor/broker		
Insurance agent/policy (life)		
Insurance agent/policy (home)		
Insurance agent/policy (auto)		
Insurance agent/policy (disability)		
Employee pension plan		
Passports		
Income tax returns		
PINs, IDs and passwords		

My power of attorney is: ______________________

My executor/executrix is: ______________________

Note: Remember to also check beneficiaries on RRSP and other registered plans, life insurance documents, employee pensions, life insurance and more. Your legal, tax and financial professionals can help you expand this checklist.

*See **www.financialdecisionsmatter.com** for a Word file of this checklist.

Records Checklist*

Permanent Records (keep for your lifetime)	✓
Birth certificate	
Marriage certificate	
Will	
Living will	
Power of Attorney (property)	
Power of Attorney (personal care)	
Social Insurance Number card(s)	
Health card(s)	
Life Insurance policy	
Home Insurance policy	
Auto Insurance policy	
Mortgage agreement	
Line of credit agreement	
Pre-planned funeral documents	
Diplomas	

Temporary Records: Long Term (6 years for tax purposes)	✓
Income tax returns	
Child care expense receipts	
Charitable donations receipts	
Medical expenses receipts	
Spousal/child support payments	
RRSP contribution receipts	
Moving expenses	

*See **www.financialdecisionsmatter.com** for a Word file of this checklist.

Records Checklist*

Temporary Records: Short Term	✓
Utility bills	
Credit card statements	
Bank statements	
Household expense receipts	

Shred These Records!	✓
Temporary records when no longer required	
Anything with name, address, phone number, etc.	
ATM slips	

*See **www.financialdecisionsmatter.com** for a Word file of this checklist.

CHAPTER 4

IMPORTANT FINANCIAL CONVERSATIONS

The quickest way to double your money
is to fold it in half and put it in your back pocket.

—Will Rogers

Important Financial Conversations

Talking openly about money and financial issues can be more delicate than discussing politics, sex or religion. We don't always know what we don't know and can feel embarrassed or ashamed that we don't understand more about money or have more of it.

Here are a few thoughts that might make these conversations a bit easier. There's no specific script that works in all situations, but it helps to know how to start the conversation and what you might say.

Talking with Your Spouse or Partner

I'm sure you had several talks with your spouse or partner before deciding to live together or get married. Unfortunately, I know the reality is that many couples don't have "the talk" about money while they're dating and many don't really even know each other's financial situation years into their marriage (how much debt each has, assets, each other's credit scores, and more).

Having this conversation can be tricky for some couples. When I've covered this subject on TV, some reporters have accused me (half-jokingly) of starting a fight as opposed to a conversation. True, this subject can be a point of contention in one's relationship, but understanding each other's thoughts, feelings and goals can't be neglected. In the long term, getting on the same page financially, or at least understanding each other better, is necessary in any partnership.

Add to the delicacy of the subject the possibility that one partner may be in a second or third marriage. Perhaps one spouse has children from another relationship and the other doesn't. One may have been "burned" financially by another spouse and be very closed about the entire subject. If that is the case, and you know bringing up finances with your significant other will be uncomfortable or too difficult to handle, consider consulting a professional. If you have an accountant, banker

Getting on the same page financially, or at least understanding each other better, is necessary in any partnership.

or financial planner whom you trust, having that third party bring up the challenging details might be the best way to start and the most comfortable approach for both of you.

However, most couples would like to get on the same page with their partner, but just don't know where to start. I've devised six steps to ease you into talking about your life goals and explain how to get there with your partner. If you're flying solo, try the exercises anyway as they're still worthwhile even without the dialogue part. But remember, it's not a task you should do and then shelve and never think about it again, but this should be a process which is fun and revealing. Take your time and enjoy the financial clarity you'll create.

The Six-Step Conversation

Things that are this important cannot be settled in one date night. You will need several conversations to get everything onto the table and discussed. Both of you need to do a lot of soul-searching to be completely honest with yourselves and each other about what your goals and expectations are in both the short and long term. Even with the best of intentions, realizing and putting words to your dreams can be very difficult and require a great deal of patience from each of you.

Step 1: What Are Our Goals?

Ease into your first financial conversation. You might say to your significant other:

> I've been reading this book on financial basics and it got me wondering about what's important in your life. We haven't really spoken about that before. And the author suggested we book a date night, even if it's just 30 minutes, and brainstorm our short-, medium- and long-term goals. Let's book a night when we can find some time together.

The purpose of this Step is to get a clear idea of each other's goals for the next one to ten years. If either of you doesn't have a clear idea, here are some conversation starters:

Housing

- save up for a home
- upgrade our home and/or appliances
- renovate our home
- buy a cottage
- be mortgage free
- build a secondary suite

Children

- start having children and when
- have more children and when
- start saving for the kids education
- assist the kids with buying their first home, car, etc.
- maternity/paternity leave

Education/Sabbaticals

- upgrading education and when
- part-time education and when
- sabbatical, when, length of time

Travel

- where/when

Obviously the list could go on. Don't feel you need to address everything in one sitting. This should be a living document that you and your spouse or family add to over the coming months and review twice a year. Don't be concerned with very short-term goals as we address them in Step 2.

Step 2: Needs and Wants List

This step can be a great deal of fun. Again, you may wish to try this exercise over a date night or at least in a relaxing setting, possibly over a glass of wine. Get a blank sheet of paper and each of you should complete your "wants" and "needs" list for the next 3, 6 and 12 months. Compare each list and agree on one pick from each category (one want, one need) that you'll both tackle first together. You might be surprised what each of you thought was a want and what truly was a need.

Step 3: Where Are We Now?

Next, start with where you are as a team. Gather all your debts, assets in as much detail as possible. This step might take a few days to several weeks for you both to complete. You'll also want to find out as much about your assets as possible, such as the approximate value of your home if you own one, how much each of you has in an RRSP or TFSA (we'll cover tax shelters in **Chapter 8**), what any non-registered accounts are valued at, what were your rates of return last year, etc.

Step 4: How Are We Going To Get To Our Goals?

This is where you as a couple need to do a little number-crunching. A good place to start is on the website of your financial institution. Once you've both determined your top goals and chosen a need you want to work toward, you'll need to figure out how to get there. Here are some ideas:

- emergency savings
- saving up for a home
- affording your home
- pay down the mortgage vs. investing in an RRSP or TFSA
- vacations vs. renovations
- kids' education vs. your own advanced education
- sabbaticals vs. maternity or paternity leave

Step 5: Make Changes

If you're going to achieve something different from what you both have now, what changes need to be made? Giving up something to fast-track saving for the down payment of your first house? Giving up buying your lunch at work in exchange for a beach holiday next year? Perhaps one spouse is willing to work overtime while the other goes back for a master's degree. Again, this Step may take weeks or even months. Revisit this area often, even if it's just a short conversation about your progress thus far or to reset time frames and priorities.

Step 6: Take Action and Get Help

Make a list of what needs to be done next: for example, get a mortgage, prepare your wills, etc.

For help in finding a financial professional to help you reach your goals, see **Talking to the Professionals** later in the chapter.

The Six-Step Conversation

Step 1: What Are Our Goals?
Step 2: Needs and Wants List
Step 3: Where Are We Now?
Step 4: How Are We Going To Get To Our Goals?
Step 5: Make Changes
Step 6: Take Action and Get Help

Talking with Your Kids

People often ask me how soon they should start talking about money and finance with their kids. I'll bring it back to matters of health. It should be a daily priority to make enlightened decisions about our health and talk about those decisions in our daily conversations with our children of any age. But when it comes to matters of money, many people have funny feelings and past histories concerning a lack of money and/or education. On a subject that embarrasses us to even think about, we probably have no idea where to begin teaching our kids. In fact, we probably have no idea where to begin solving the problem for ourselves. But I assure you that you're not alone and you only need a healthy curiosity to work these issues out successfully. Plus, if you're lacking in financial knowledge, think how wonderful it will be for your child not to grow up with the same lack of understanding about something so fundamentally important to the day-to-day dealings of our lives—money.

Learn While You Teach

A great beginning is simply to be interested in the topic yourself. Put on your student hat. Give yourself permission to learn as you teach your children. Keep in mind that even at a precious young age, kids hear what we say and keenly tune into our body language. You'll want to be cautious not to use emotional adjectives when describing money such as filthy, dirty, good or bad. Money should never be used as a reward or punishment for good or bad behaviour, just as experts tell us not to use food in that way. Of course a convenient source of information exists right at your fingertips in your computer. Consider a field trip with your child to the library or bookstore. Get a money book such as the CICA's *A Parent's Guide to Raising Money-Smart Kids* (to order an eBook or download a pdf, go to **www.financialdecisionsmatter.com**) or other books written especially for educating kids—they tend to have a surreptitious way of educating parents at the same time.

Talking with Your Parents

If you're blessed enough to still have one or both parents in your life, this can be the most difficult conversation of all. I realize that for some families it's simply not possible as they are very "closed" about money. My husband came from one such family. In my own family, we've always been extremely open about matters of money, debt and specific wishes at death. Because I come from an extremely large family with many older members, I've attended at least one funeral each year since I was a small child, I've also had to plan a number of them. I know one thing for sure; the death of a family member is one of the most difficult times in your life. Dealing with our own emotions as well as trying to carry out the wishes of our parents at the time of their passing is very stressful. This is a time when you want important information to be easily accessible. Knowing where everything is and being able to carry out their wishes takes a huge amount of pressure off the family and the person planning the funeral.

For families such as my husband's, "the talk" might never happen. For my family, it happens far too often for my liking. But for most, there's a healthy in-between. It's not a conversation you need to have often; a brief exchange once in a while can save so much future grief and needless worry.

CICA has published an excellent book which covers all the aspects of financial decisions for end of life planning. It includes practical information and checklists to guide you. To download a free eBook or pdf, please go to **www.financialdecisionsmatter.com**.

Talking with the Professionals

At some time you are going to want to or need to talk with a financial planner, a lawyer and an insurance agent. But what should you ask them in order to get the service you need? The following are taken from conversations I have had with professionals in these fields.

Important Issues to Discuss with Your Financial Planner

With Ken Costello, President and CEO of the Canadian Institute of Financial Planners

Kelley: How do I find a financial planner?

Ken: The best way is by referral from a trusted friend or family member. You can also find a planner in good standing on the Financial Planning Standards Council (FPSC) website (see **www.fpsc.ca** and the **Resources** chapter at the end of this book).

Kelley: What should I ask myself before going to a financial planner?

Ken: Am I ready to truly commit to an engagement with a financial planner and meet my obligations as part of that relationship (e.g., disclosing personal information, providing up-to-date information, meeting regularly, etc.)? What objective am I trying to achieve by dealing with a planner (e.g., tax strategies, investment advice, etc.)?

Kelley: What are the top four questions I should ask a financial planner?

Ken:

1. What are your qualifications? Do you have any professional designations? What are they, and how do they apply to my particular situation?
2. Do you follow the six-step financial planning process? (See the **Resources** chapter at the end of this book for a link to the six steps you should expect).
3. What are the areas in which you specialize?
4. How are you compensated? (I would add, "If I left you tomorrow and hired another advisor, what would that cost me?").

Kelley: What should I look out for?

Ken: Relevant qualifications (e.g., experience, professional designations, etc.). Does the planner practise full financial planning or do they focus on just selling products? How often has the planner committed to meet me each year? Will the planner enter into a client-planner engagement? Will the planner be able to address all my needs or will I have to work with other people as well (e.g., insurance agents, estate planners, tax planners, investment specialists, etc.)? I would also ask them what products they are licensed to sell.

Important Issues to Discuss with Your Lawyer

With Yolanda Van Wachem of McLennan Ross LLP

Kelley: What are the top three things in my financial life that I should seek from a lawyer?

Yolanda: The major documents to consider are wills, powers of attorney and prenuptial agreements.

With wills, ensure that you review them often. This is not a document to get done and never look at again. If a will is drafted when their children are young, most couples aren't concerned as much about assets as they are about guardianship of the children. Fast forward 10 or 20 years, and the situation is likely dramatically different.

You'll want to ensure you also have a living will (often also called a personal care directive) in place.

Powers of attorney are one of the most important documents your legal professional can draft. They're not expensive and everyone should have them in place. A power of attorney lists who can and will make financial decisions on your behalf if needed (i.e., if you were on an extended vacation) and also, if there was a temporary or permanent mental incapacity. If these documents are not in existence in a time of need, the cost can be enormous.

If you are getting married, consider a prenuptial agreement. A co-habitation agreement should be considered if you are planning to live together but not marry.

Kelley: What should I ask myself before seeking legal services concerning my finances? What should I look out for?

Yolanda: Be cautious about adding a spouse, child or someone else as a joint owner of any asset. Doing so could mean losing not only control, but could create tax and other consequences. If you are transferring property or funds, carefully think through all tax, legal and other considerations and seek legal advice.

Keep in mind situations where you don't want to act without legal counsel: buying and selling a home, opening a small business, allowing someone to live in your home (therefore possibly becoming a dependant) and more.

Important Issues to Discuss with Your Life Insurance Agent

With Greg Pollock, President and CEO of Advocis, The Financial Advisors Association of Canada

Kelley: What are the top three things the average person should know about life insurance?

Greg: The first thing people need to understand about individual life insurance is that its purpose is to ensure family members and loved ones are financially protected in the event of one's death. Life insurance can provide funds for things such as funeral expenses, paying down debt or providing an income for dependants.

The second thing is that a life insurance policy is a contractual agreement between you and a life insurance company that guarantees payment of the face value of the policy upon death. There are many options when it comes to choosing a policy that makes the most sense for you and your family. A financial advisor who is licensed to sell life insurance can help you select the product that best suits your needs. He or she will conduct a needs analysis that addresses your financial situation, and will then document current and future goals to develop an individualized financial plan to achieve those goals.

As part of the financial planning process, a good financial advisor will explain products and options to help you arrive at an informed decision. He or she will help answer questions to determine the type of coverage needed (i.e., short-term, permanent or a mix of the two), how much insurance is needed and whether other types of insurance, such as disability or critical illness, are also required. If you're self-employed, for example, and become disabled and are unable to work, disability insurance can provide you with the funds needed to pay expenses. Critical illness insurance helps pay costs associated with life-altering illnesses.

The third thing to know is that as your circumstances change, your level of life insurance coverage may also need to change. Therefore your policies should be reviewed with your advisor regularly, or as your situation changes. Life insurance is an essential part of a comprehensive financial plan that helps consumers prepare for every eventuality.

Kelley: What should I ask myself before buying life insurance?

Greg: One of the first questions is, "Am I dealing with an advisor who is a member of a professional association?" I've already mentioned that members of Advocis must abide by a strict code of ethics, but they are also required to uphold standards of best practice, participate in ongoing continuing education programs, and maintain appropriate levels of professional liability insurance. Belonging to a professional association and adhering to its membership requirements demonstrates a commitment by the advisor to always work within the best interests of the client. (See **www.advocis.ca** and the **Resources** chapter.)

Kelley: What should I look out for when shopping for life insurance?

Greg: An insurance-licensed financial advisor will help you sort through the maze of options available. Whether it's a whole life, universal life, term to 100 or a term policy, each type of insurance has its own set of features. It's important that your compare these features to ensure you understand the pros and cons of each.

Some features to consider include: whether the policy is renewable (meaning you can renew your policy at the end of its term, in the case of term insurance, for a higher premium without submitting to a medical examination), or if it's convertible (meaning you have the option of exchanging your term policy for a permanent insurance policy without submitting to a medical examination); death benefits; premiums; cash values and other significant features.

Kelley: What should I look for when dealing with a life insurance agent?

Greg: The most important thing is to ensure that the advisor is a licensed professional. In addition to asking the advisor if they belong to a professional association such as Advocis or another association, ask about the advisor's professional qualifications and training. Look for someone who holds the CLU (Chartered Life Underwriter) designation or the CHS (Certified Health Specialist) designation, which demonstrates a commitment to their professional development. Finally, work with someone you trust. It's important that you feel comfortable with your financial advisor or life insurance agent as this is the person who will help you navigate your financial future.

Kelley: What are three trouble signs I should watch for?

Greg: With the exception of Quebec, currently the use of the words "financial planner" and "financial advisor" are not regulated in Canada. Be sure you are dealing with a qualified professional who has the credentials and education necessary to assist you with your insurance needs. Don't be afraid to interview several advisors and ask for references from other clients. Avoid anyone who tries to sell you a particular plan or product and won't suggest alternatives—there is likely more than one solution to your life insurance needs.

In addition, the Canadian Life and Health Insurance Association (CLHIA) also recommends you ask for proposals in writing (policy illustrations), and that you watch out for any suggestion that you surrender your present policies. Certainly, there are some occasions when a replacement policy is in a client's best interest; but there are also occasions when it is not. If you already have a policy in place, weigh the pros and cons of both your current and proposed policies. It may be possible to alter your existing policy to meet your current needs. Again, if you are working with an advisor who belongs to a professional association, that person is subject to a strict code of professional conduct and therefore should always be putting the client's needs first.

In addition, once you've decided to purchase a policy, be sure to read the application form *carefully* and *thoroughly* before signing. Your signature authorizes the insurance company to confirm your medical history on a confidential basis. Once the policy is delivered, your advisor should review it with you to ensure this is the policy you bought. Working with a professional insurance or financial advisor will help you avoid costly mistakes and ensure the decision you make with respect to your policy is an informed one.

Please note: when it comes to matters of your finances, never be afraid to ask how, and how much, a financial advisor or insurance sales person is being paid for the products and/or services they're recommending.

Negotiating Outside the Family

So few of us in Canada take pleasure or even try to negotiate a better price unless we're travelling in a country where it's part of the culture. Negotiating doesn't need to be laborious or require the skills of a master sales person. It's simply asking to get a little more or to pay a bit less. Why leave money on the table? Why not get a free upgrade or gift of appreciation for shopping at the same place you always do? What about a discount if your family frequents the same establishments? Simply asking, "What's your best offer?" or "What else can you throw in or do for me?" and then remaining quiet can work wonders. You won't succeed every time and you may have to be prepared to walk away and try again. But negotiating could save you countless thousands of dollars over a lifetime or get you more than you ever imagined. Plus, it can be contagious and fun if you make it seem like a game. Be sure to explain the process and what you're trying to achieve when your children are with you as well.

Here are some areas in your life to ask for a deal:

- your **cell, phone, Internet and cable company:** call every three to six months just to see what new offers they have
- a **restaurant** that you and your family frequent
- **furniture and appliance stores**: ask if the store honours future sale prices for, say, 30 days; if you're purchasing a big-ticket item such as a TV, a future sale could save you a lot of money later
- **car and home insurance** for better rates
- **credit card companies** for a better rate on the interest you pay if you carry a balance each month
- **banks** to waive some fees if you have three or more products or give you a better rate on your mortgage or GICs
- **independent stores** for gifts with purchases—especially if the store is competing with the big box stores; an owner is much more likely to want to keep you as a return customer; it can be as simple as asking, "What else can you throw in with my purchase, for a good customer?"
- **trades people** doing renovations or service work of any kind
- **student's or senior's discount** or even the GST or HST off
- **volume discount for anything**.

Negotiating is simply asking to get a little more or to pay a bit less.

I'm not suggesting that you go overboard looking for deals and clipping coupons (unless you like to do that), and be careful that you don't buy a product or service just because you have a coupon for it. You also need to factor in what your time is worth and ensure you're not running around town for a better deal when you could have been paid much more for overtime at work, for example.

Disputes

Equally as difficult, if not more so, is dispute resolution. Whether it's an error on your utility bill or you were promised a better rate on your cell phone plan and never received it, it's your right as a consumer to get what is fair or what you were promised. However, dealing with some companies can feel hopeless and far too many consumers just give up.

If you are calling a company to complain or resolve an issue, ask for a supervisor or manager immediately. Also, try to call during regular business hours (usually Monday to Friday, 9am–5pm) even if they're open evenings and weekends. Generally, senior staff (such as managers) get the best shifts and usually have the most power. Someone working at a call centre at 9pm on a Saturday night is likely to be an employee with little authority to get things done.

If none of your methods resolve the matter, try the following when escalating your complaint:

- your local Better Business Bureau
- if it's a dispute with a bank or trust company, the Ombudsman
- if it's a dispute with someone in the financial industry such as a financial advisor, try their regulatory body or the Office of Consumer Affairs.

(See the **Resources** chapter at the end of the book for contact information.)

The Government of Canada also has an excellent website detailing where to direct your complaints, and also the rights you have as a consumer in the area of banking, mortgages, credit and much more.

Easy Action Steps

1. **Set a date night with your spouse or yourself and list your short, medium and long-term financial goals and dreams.**
2. **Have the financial "talk" with your kids, parents and siblings.**
3. **Pick one opportunity this week to negotiate a deal or ask for more.**

CHAPTER 5

UNDERSTANDING YOUR MORTGAGE

A bank is a place that will lend you money
if you can prove that you don't need it.

—Bob Hope

Understanding Your Mortgage

Canadians who buy their own home today expect to have a mortgage. With the cost of houses so high and current mortgage interest rates historically low, this is not too surprising. There are, however, many things to think about before making that purchase. Even your peer group can influence your decision. Do your friends own homes? Do they have huge houses with huge mortgages, or are they dedicated to paying their mortgages down or off and are happy to stay put in the more modest, but affordable, house. Whatever your decision, it is essential that you understand how mortgages can work for you to help you make the biggest and most important purchase of your life.

My "Gut Reaction" Test

There are times in your financial life when "numbers" are presented to you in the form of two or more options (of course, not doing anything is always one option!). The numbers might make sense on paper for you to move in one direction, but your gut reaction, nervous tummy or "sleep at night" factor doesn't work with these choices. Listen to your gut reaction because it's generally a pretty accurate gauge of what's right for you.

This is particularly important when it comes to buying a house and taking on a mortgage, but the best instincts in the world won't help much if you don't understand some basics about long-term debt and mortgages.

Listen to your gut reaction because it's generally a pretty accurate gauge of what's right for you.

Terminology

There is some terminology you must understand before embarking on the biggest and most important purchase of your life.

Mortgage

A mortgage is a loan secured by real property, i.e., land and buildings. If you buy a house by taking out a mortgage loan, you sign a contract obligating you to pay off the loan over a period of time, usually 25 years. The mortgage contract includes an interest rate and a schedule of payments called an amortization schedule.

Amortization

The amortization period is the length of time required to repay the mortgage loan in full. This is when you make regular payments combining interest and principal according to a timetable. Most financial institutions offer weekly, bi-weekly, semi-monthly and monthly payment options. Keep in mind that the amortization is simply an estimate of what payment amounts would be paid if the interest rate remained fixed for the full length of the mortgage (say 25 years) and the payments remained constant as well. The amortization period is usually broken up into five-year terms when a certain interest rate can apply.

Term

The term is the period (usually five years) during which the mortgage interest rate is in effect.

Variable-Rate Mortgage

A variable-rate mortgage has an interest rate that may change during the term of the mortgage. The interest rate is usually a certain per cent above the bank's prime rate.

Fixed-Rate Mortgage

A fixed-rate mortgage has the same interest rate for the entire term. Amortization schedules for fixed-rate mortgages stay the same for the full term. The term for a short-term fixed-rate mortgage can be as short as a year and as long as 10 years for a longer-term mortgage.

Your Biggest Expense

Your mortgage will no doubt be your biggest monthly expense. The amount of your mortgage payment is determined by the price of the house, the rate you were able to negotiate with the lender and your payment schedule. Having too big a mortgage payment for your available cash can be absolutely crippling. You should be especially careful if you stretch your finances to get into an expensive house at a time of low mortgage rates and high house prices.

As you have probably noticed, the relation between house prices and mortgage rates is inverse, i.e., the lower the mortgage rate, the more people seem to be willing to pay for houses, which then drives house prices up. In some markets the demand for houses exceeds the supply, which causes bidding wars and house prices to rise. As a result of these factors, buyers pay more to buy the house and have large mortgages at low interest rates. But even at low rates, ownership of a house can still require a lot of cash for the monthly payment. Then what happens at the end of five years when the mortgage rate has to be renegotiated? A jump from 4% to 6% in the rate will increase your monthly mortgage payments by 50%.

The lesson here is to look ahead. When buying a house, do the math and figure out what monthly payment you can afford now and also what you will be able to afford if rates are higher when you have to renegotiate. The bank websites have calculators that can be very valuable in giving you an idea of what you can afford, but they should be used as a guide only. The details of your own particular situation, however, will have to be worked out with your lender.

When buying a house, do the math and figure out what monthly payment you can afford now and also what you will be able to afford if rates are higher when you have to renegotiate.

Mortgage Payments

Regular payments combining interest and principal are made according to a timetable:

- in the early years of the mortgage, most of each payment is interest
- later, this reverses itself until most of each payment is principal

- financial institutions allow lump-sum payments every year without penalty
- if you wish to pay off the entire mortgage ahead of schedule, a significant penalty is usually charged (three month's interest is common) so the bank can recover some of the interest it would have collected if the mortgage had run its full term
- banks renegotiate the interest rate at the end of each term within the schedule to reflect rates prevailing at that time (a common term is five years).

If you fail to make the payments, the bank can foreclose, i.e., force a sale of the property in order to try to recover the unpaid remainder of its loan.

Canadian Home Ownership

According to the May 2012 report *Confidence in the Canadian Mortgage Market*[1] published by the Canadian Association of Accredited Mortgage Professionals (CAAMP):

- there are about 13.7 million households in Canada
- 9.6 million Canadians own their own homes
- 5.85 million have mortgages
- the average outstanding principal is $170,000
- the average mortgage interest rate is 3.64%
- more than 600,000 homes were purchased in 2011
- the average mortgage amount was $224,000
- approximately 65% of mortgage holders have fixed-rate mortgages
- on average, owners with mortgages have about 49% equity in their homes
- in the last year about 18% of those with mortgages have used their equity as a source of funds for renovations, education, debt consolidation and repayment, and purchases of various kinds.

Paying Down the Mortgage

CAAMP reports that most borrowers are paying down their mortgages faster than required under their mortgage contracts. About half of all households are paying $100 or more per month more than the contracted amount. Despite the cash available in many households to accelerate paying off the mortgage, a study released in May 2012 by BMO Financial Group indicated that 51% of

1 **http://caamp.org/meloncms/media/Spring%20Report%202012_ENG.pdf**

Canadian homeowners expect to carry a mortgage into retirement and 52% say the burden of their mortgages is preventing them from saving for retirement.

If you have been contributing regularly to an RRSP over the years but you are approaching retirement and still have a mortgage, you should seriously consider your options to speed up the mortgage amortization. The banks have become very flexible about mortgage payments. They will allow you to increase the amount of each payment, pay more frequently and allow you to make large payments each year without penalty. As noted in the CAAMP report previously, many people are taking advantage of this flexibility to reduce the amortization period and thereby reduce the amount of interest they have to pay.

Seriously consider your options to speed up the mortgage amortization. The banks have become very flexible about mortgage payments.

Preparing to Buy

Let's suppose you want to buy a house or condominium. The best place to start is the Canada Mortgage and Housing Corporation (CMHC) website: **www.cmhc.ca/en/index.cfm**.

CMHC provides mortgage insurance, mortgage-backed securities, develops housing policy for the federal government and does research.

On its website, the section "Homebuying Step by Step" is very valuable to anyone thinking of buying a home because it forces you to look at the fundamentals:

- the buy/rent decision
- your finances
- what kind of home is right for you
- the buying process

There is also a glossary and a very useful set of worksheets that let you "crunch" your own numbers to let you work out what is best for you within your household income.

The websites of the major banks also provide useful information, especially about mortgage rates. They have calculators that allow you to work out a payment schedule for your mortgage. These figures will show you the affordability of the home you want to own.

Insurance

Insurance is really important to protect what is probably the largest investment of your life. You want to protect your property against loss, and you want to make sure the mortgage will be paid and your family will be able to continue living in their home if you die or are incapacitated.

A new type of threat against your ownership has surfaced in recent years: theft of your home through someone stealing your identity and selling your home without you even knowing about it.

In Canada today, there are four main kinds of insurance that affect your mortgage and ownership of your home. Two are mandatory under certain conditions and the other two are optional and should be considered:

- Title insurance (optional)
- Homeowner's insurance
- Mortgage (life) insurance (optional)
- CMHC mortgage insurance.

Title Insurance

If you're buying a house, title insurance is really worth considering. It is designed to protect you against any dispute over ownership of your property. Clear title, i.e., ownership, is essential for you to have the right to live on your property and sell it. You are also protected against anything revealed by a subsequent survey, such as an easement (right of way across your property), encroachment (a claim by a neighbour that they have title to land that extends into yours) or a claim by a missing heir of a previous owner to an interest in your property.

One important area of protection is title theft by an identity thief. By acquiring your identity through stealing your personal information, the thief sells or remortgages your property without your knowledge. The fraudster takes the mortgage money or the proceeds from the sale of your house. The loss is borne by you and your lender. Although home ownership identity theft cases are relatively rare, they do happen and it can be a very expensive, time-consuming and traumatic ordeal to prove your ownership if it happens to you. The cost of the policy is very reasonable (usually about $250 to $300) and well worth it. The premium is a one-time payment that buys coverage for as long as you own the house. Your lawyer will offer it to you when you purchase your home.

Identity Theft Can Happen to Houses?

An elderly man rented a property to a tenant who forged a power of attorney for property in the name of the man's non-existent "grandson". Using this power of attorney, the fraudster-tenant listed the house for sale and sold it without the knowledge of the true owner. At closing, a bank advanced mortgage money to the new owner through his lawyer. The lawyer drew a certified cheque on his trust account in favour of the true owner. The "grandson" using his power of attorney forged the true owner's name, deposited the purchase money in the "grandson's" account and disappeared. It took two court hearings to get title restored to the true owner. Lawsuits involving the lawyer, the bank that issued the cheque with the forged name and the title insurer resulted in the bank having to reimburse the title company which had honoured the claim under the purchaser's title insurance policy and paid the mortgage lender for its loss.

Homeowner's Insurance

There is a wide range of policies for houses, condos, cottages, etc., but the bottom line is that your large investment is protected against any major loss by fire, theft, vandalism, some types of water damage, and liability if someone is injured on your premises. If you don't have insurance, a large loss can wipe you out, so it is highly recommended.

Homeowner's insurance is mandatory if you have or are applying for a mortgage. You must prove to your mortgage lender that you have insurance on your mortgaged property, or the lender won't give you a mortgage. The lender's name is always included on the policy to protect their financial interest.

Homeowner's insurance is mandatory if you have or are applying for a mortgage.

Mortgage (Life) Insurance

You can buy another type of mortgage insurance called mortgage life insurance to pay off the mortgage if the policyholder (you) dies before the mortgage is completely paid off. Premiums can be expensive and are based on the borrower's age and other factors. It's best to ask your financial institution to provide some numbers to see if this option is worthwhile for you.

CMHC Mortgage Insurance

CMHC (Canada Mortgage and Housing Corporation) insurance is mandatory if you are applying for a mortgage with a down payment of less than 20% of the purchase price. It is required by CMHC as protection for the lender in case the homeowner defaults. The idea is that if a person invests at least 20% of the value of the house as a down payment, if bad times hit (i.e., housing prices drop—as they did dramatically in the U.S. over the past few years—and/or if interest rates rose), those with larger down payments would have a cushion of equity (protecting the bank from the owner owing more than the value of the home) and also protecting the investment of the borrower. If the borrower's down payment is less than 20%, they must pay for the CMHC insurance. The cost depends on the size of the down payment, i.e., insurance is much higher if you have a 5% down payment and much lower if you have 15%. The insurance rate is also dependent on other factors, such as the borrower's employment status.

This could be an incentive to wait and save for a down payment that is large enough to avoid paying these additional high costs.

How to Buy a House

The following cases show how two couples wanted to buy their first homes. We look at the factors they had to face and what they found out about what it takes to get the home of your dreams.

Buying a House—Welcome to Our New Home

Joseph and Andrea are an average Canadian couple in their early 30s who want to buy a house and start a family, but they aren't sure what they can afford. They both earn the average Canadian salary of $46,194 reported by Statistics Canada in its March 2012 survey of "Payroll Employment, Earnings and Hours". This gives their two-person household a total gross income of $92,388. They are prudent in their spending habits. Their car is eight years old, but it is paid for. Neither has a university degree and therefore no large student loans to pay off. They have no personal line of credit and a limit on their credit card of only $5,000. Between the two of them they have managed to save $50,000 for a down payment.

Joseph and Andrea know that mortgage rates are at or near historic lows and are able to negotiate a 3.5% variable rate, a good rate because of their high credit score. They do all their banking at the same bank so have a bit of negotiating power to get a better mortgage rate than that posted on their bank's website. They choose a variable rate rather than a 5.24% fixed rate because they feel interest rates are unlikely to rise sufficiently over the five-year term to justify locking in at 5.24% today. The 3.5% rate passed the "gut reaction test" and Joseph and Andrea feel they can sleep comfortably at night taking this risk. However, if the floating rate rises to the point where Joseph and Andrea begin to worry that it could rise even higher and decide to lock in, they will have to lock in at the then prevailing fixed mortgage rate, which could be well above 5.24%.

...continued

They've filled out the CMHC worksheets and used the mortgage payment calculator on their bank's website to work their numbers. Here's what they came up with:

• maximum purchase price	$401,038
• down payment	$50,000
• term	5 years
• amortization period	25 years
• mortgage principal amount	$351,038
• CMHC insurance premium	$7,021
• total mortgage amount	$358,059
• interest rate	3.5%
• monthly mortgage payment	$1,758
• total monthly housing costs (including mortgage)	$2,464

What Can We Afford?

From working these numbers, Joseph and Andrea can get an indication of what they can afford to buy and what they can afford to carry each month. The surprise is that they can afford a house above the national average price of $375,810 but their $50,000 down payment is still only 12.5% of the purchase price. As a result they have to buy expensive CMHC mortgage insurance.

Joseph and Andrea also have the option of changing their mortgage payment from monthly to semi-monthly, bi-weekly or weekly. By paying more frequently or paying a larger amount per payment they can reduce the amortization period. By paying $448.14 weekly, for example, they could save about $24,661 in interest costs over the full 25-year amortization, and take three years off the amortization period compared to their current plan to pay monthly. Banks also allow lump sum payments

...continued

during the year. The usual amount is 15% of the total mortgage amount per year. In the case of Joseph and Andrea, that would be $52,656 per year they could pay off if they could afford it. If they get a windfall, they could pay off the entire amount of the mortgage at the end of the fifth year without penalty. At the end of the five-year term, Joseph and Andrea will have to decide whether they want to lock into a fixed mortgage or take the risk again of the variable (also referred to as floating) rate offered by the bank at that time.

Comparing 25-Year Amortization Against 15-Year

Joseph and Andrea want to consider all their options, so they ask the financial institution to provide some numbers for a 15-year amortization, so they can compare it against the 25-year amortization.

If they choose the 25-year amortization, they will pay $21,089 to carry their mortgage in the first year, of which $12,011 will be interest, so they will actually pay off only $8,945 of the principal price of the house.

If they choose the 15-year amortization, their monthly payments would jump to $2,510 per month, but they would save $75,502 in interest costs if they shortened the amortization period to 15 years from 25.

Buying a House—Maybe We Should Wait

Ethan and Isabelle are excited about buying their first house. They really want to buy as soon as possible but aren't sure if they saved up enough money. They went to their bank's website and crunched some numbers on the bank's easy-to-use calculators. They have their eye on a house listed at $400,000 and want to know whether they could buy it on their incomes and with their other expenses. They have an $80,000 down payment saved after years of scrimping.

...continued

What Can They Afford?

Here are the personal statistics the bank looks at to help in its estimate of what the couple can afford.

Salary

- Ethan $55,000
- Isabelle $45,000

Car loan

- principal $31,000
- monthly payment $556

Line of credit

- Ethan $10,000 to pay off a student loan

VISA balance

- Isabelle $5,000

The bank's posted rate is 5.44% for a fixed rate mortgage with a five-year term. If they choose to pay bi-weekly to speed up the amortization, they will have to pay $896.35 every two weeks. The total interest costs over the five-year term would be $81,188.15. Their banker tells them that by locking into a five-year fixed-rate mortgage they will be paying 5.44% for five years and that if they want to leave their bank or opt for a different type of mortgage, they will have to pay a penalty.

For Ethan and Isabelle, the floating rate mortgage failed the "gut reaction test". They would be very uncomfortable worrying that rates might go up. They would sooner pay a higher rate now than risk having to pay an even higher rate if interest rates climbed and took mortgage rates above 5.44%.

...continued

Even though Ethan and Isabelle have an $80,000 down payment, they are not as lucky as Joseph and Andrea. Ethan and Isabelle can only afford a purchase price of $367,250 because their estimated monthly housing costs of $2,377 (including heating of $175 and property taxes of $459) would make it impossible for them to pay the bi-weekly mortgage payments.

Ethan and Isabelle are $32,750 short of their dream. What are the options now? They could consider the following:

- wait until they have a larger down payment
- earn extra income by purchasing a property with an income suite
- consider a longer amortization and monthly payments
- consider a smaller house or buying in the suburbs at a lower price.

Using Your RRSP for a Down Payment

If you are a first-time buyer, you can take funds out of your RRSP to use for a down payment on a house under the Home Buyer's Plan (HBP). However, there are some conditions which apply:

- Each of you, your spouse or your common-law partner, can withdraw up to $25,000 per year from your own plan to buy or build a home (provided you are first-time buyers).
- You can also withdraw money to buy or build a house for a related person with a disability.
- The withdrawn money is not included in your taxable income in the year withdrawn.
- Your RRSP contributions must remain in the RRSP for at least 90 days before you can withdraw them under the HBP, or they may not be deductible for any year.
- You must repay something every year until the full amount is repaid within 15 years.

Contribute to an RRSP or Pay Down the Mortgage?

This is the great debate. The ideal, of course, is to have a mortgage-free retirement and live on the returns of a sizeable RRSP, other non-registered investments and, hopefully, a company pension. Since most people's resources are limited by their earnings, mortgage payments or RRSP contributions often become competing priorities.

Since retirement is a time to enjoy life with a minimum of obligations, let's assume you want to have the mortgage paid off before you retire. Since mortgage payments are not tax deductible in Canada, taxable withdrawals from an RRSP to pay a mortgage can quickly eat into savings. Even tax-free withdrawals from a TFSA also reduce savings but at a slower rate.

The four key factors to consider in deciding whether to pay down the mortgage or contribute to your RRSP are:

- the rate of interest you are paying on your mortgage
- the number of years left to pay off the mortgage
- the rate of return you are getting on your RRSP
- your personal tax rate.

If your personal tax rate is high and the rate of return on your RRSP is greater than your mortgage rate, you could make your RRSP contribution and use any tax refund as a lump sum payment to reduce your mortgage.

As there are a number of complicated factors involved in this decision, as with all financial decisions, I recommend you consult your financial and/or tax professional.

Easy Action Steps

Each year when your mortgage statement comes in, dedicate a little time to ensuring you're aware of your options and if you should make any changes.

Take a few moments and call up your mortgage lender:

1. Have rates changed since you first took out your mortgage?
2. Should you switch from a monthly to bi-weekly (or bi-weekly to weekly) accelerated payment schedule?
3. How many years might that burn off your mortgage?

CHAPTER 6

MANAGING YOUR CASH, CREDIT CARDS AND OTHER DEBT

Too many people spend money they haven't earned, to buy things they don't want, to impress people they don't like.

— Will Smith

Managing Your Cash, Credit Cards and Other Debt

Our ability to take on debt can change our status in today's society. In our grandparents' generation, for example, you only owned what you were able to pay for. You either built a house yourself, waited decades (if ever) to afford one, or lived with your parents until either you saved enough to buy your own place, or waited until you inherited. Ego couldn't get in the way during those years. You couldn't show off things you didn't own outright. Today cars, houses, TVs, laptops and practically anything else you can name are often purchased through some credit arrangement. Vacations, dinners out, extra-curricular activities for kids are all "affordable" now because of lines of credit.

Cash

It has often been said that if you want to curtail your spending, use cash. Cash is tangible. When you pay with cash you feel a loss. Cash makes you think. Paying with plastic happens so quickly you don't feel any loss. Those who are great with cash are usually great with their credit too!

Paying with cash is becoming increasingly less common. My favourite downtown parking garage now only accepts credit cards as payment, as do airlines and many other businesses. Let's try to understand the full role of cash in our lives.

Keep Some Cash in Your House

A few years ago Toronto suffered a severe and frightening black-out, which lasted more than two days. Because there was no power, many people ran out of cash because they couldn't withdraw money from the bank machines and they also couldn't use their debit or credit cards in stores. Even though emergencies like that don't happen very often, you should keep some cash well hidden in a safe spot in your home (the amount will depend on your needs). It's also a good idea to keep some money at home in case your wallet or purse is stolen or just as a comfortable cushion. The right amount of cash to have available for an emergency is how much it would take for your family to make it through at least four days.

Household Debt

Since it's the norm today to have debt, we need to manage it well and learn to respect its impact on our lives. Debt is an important part of most household spending, so economic growth depends on household spending. When there are economic shocks, such as a rise in unemployment because of a recession, the effects on spending are significant. The main problem today is that the ratio of household debt to disposable income, i.e., after-tax income, is at a record 150%. That means that the average person would have to work for a year-and-a-half and pour all their earnings into debt reduction to clear off the debt. *A year and a half*!

Rising Consumer Debt

Up until the mid-1990s, changes in the debt-to-income ratio resulted almost solely from the growth of mortgage debt. Since that time, consumer credit has accounted for an important part of the growth, especially home equity lines of credit (HELOCs). We've enjoyed rising incomes at the same time as we've had record low interest rates and this has made mortgages more affordable. Many people have also been lucky enough to see the market value of their house continue to rise after they bought. The continued rise in house prices has increased the owner's home equity, which can be used as collateral for a HELOC.

Just Managing Your Debt is Not Enough

But how are you going to save and invest money if you pay 30% of your after-tax income to service your debt, especially when interest rates rise? You need cash today for the interest payments and you'll need even more cash in the future for the repayment of the principal. Money borrowed from the bank for consumption, car purchases, home renovations, etc., is money that cannot take advantage of investment. Many people compliment themselves on managing their debt well, i.e., never missing a payment. But, if you stop and think about it, debt, no matter how well managed, is still debt and not savings and has to be paid for and paid back.

You could manage your debt well all your life and still not have any savings.

Credit Cards

I'm not sure if it's possible to get around in today's world without a credit card. There are some people that do, but every day more and more businesses are not accepting cash or making it very difficult to pay with cash. And, if you travel, it's nearly impossible. From hotel reservations to renting a car to even booking a spa appointment or restaurant reservation, you need a credit card.

Always Carry a "Major" Credit Card

Many companies require the use of a major credit card, i.e., a bank-issued VISA, MasterCard or AMEX card. If you have a department store card or one issued by a company other than a big bank, chances are, you are not using a major credit card.

The Dangers of Department Store Cards

You know the lure: you're at a large store, maybe even making a big purchase, and you're offered 10% or more off if you take advantage of their store credit card. Should you do it? The answer is definitely "No"! While it may be tempting to save that percentage, given the extremely high interest rates department stores charge (as much as 29%) and other fees for being late, it's just not worth it. Department stores know that lending out at such high rates is big business and, if someone holds a balance all year paying 29%, why not offer a price reduction of 10% or 15%?

Even if you never carry a balance, these cards don't help your credit score and can even hurt it. We'll examine credit scores in **Chapter 7: The Importance of a Good Credit Score**.

Department store credit cards are a temptation you should resist.

Just Applying for Credit Can Hurt Your Credit Score

I covered this subject recently on a national TV show. I couldn't believe how many emails I received from viewers right across the country asking me whether getting a department store card to take advantage of store discounts, but not activating it, would affect their credit score. Many viewers said they had accepted multiple department store credit card offers for the instant discount because they thought that, if they only applied for extra credit but didn't activate the card, it would not affect their credit rating. How very wrong they were! If you apply for a credit card, your credit report will be checked. Even this simple check will count as a hit to your score, and your application will be reported as an active account *whether you've actually activated the card or not*. Please always take time to read the fine print in order to understand your potential liabilities.

If you apply for a credit card your credit report will be checked and, if you are approved, your application will be reported as an active account whether you've actually activated the card or not.

How Many Credit Cards Should You Have?

You should have more than one, but not more than three. For most people, one major VISA and MasterCard are enough. Why two? Well again, if you travel and one is shut down due to theft (and we know how quickly that can happen even if we have the physical card in our hands), it's nice to have a back-up.

Are Rewards Cards Worth the Hype?

If you're responsible with your credit cards and pay them off every month, then rewards cards can be of great value. The problem is that these cards usually have annual fees ranging from zero to $120, so be sure the reward values exceed the fee. But remember, credit card companies know that many individuals will carry a balance each month and will pay exorbitant fees for that luxury. Ensure that you're not enticed by the rewards if credit is (or has been) a problem for you.

Pros and Cons of Rewards Cards

Check that the rewards are really of value to you:

- If your travel rewards earned you $250 of travel miles per year and the annual fee is $120, you've netted $130, but $130 won't get you or your family very far.
- What's the value of a reward if it's not worth using?

Check the fine print for how and when you can redeem your points:

- Some cards allow you to use cash and points any time and with any airline
- Some have many restrictions.

The newer cash rewards cards offer cash or certificates instead of travel rewards:

- That same $130 returned to you in cash or a certificate for your favourite grocery store might be much more appreciated than having to put $130 toward a trip.

For those who make large purchases and those who are self-employed, the benefits of a rewards card can be significant:

- Some people I know have been able to take one or several family vacations per year just by having the right card and using it for all their personal and corporate purchases.

Consider the additional benefit of the protection you get by using a credit card instead of cash or debit. All credit card companies offer some protection and empowerment for you (the consumer) over the retailer. However, no protection or reward is worth carrying a balance on which you pay double-digit interest rates.

Be careful to compare annual fees, interest rates and rewards before selecting a card; you can do this with just a few Internet searches.

Should You Worry about Fraud and Theft?

You're 100% protected by the credit card companies for theft and fraud. However, you must keep your PIN protected and prove that you used your card responsibly. If you report a fraudulent purchase, the credit card company goes to the vendor and asks them to produce a receipt and compare the signature against your signature on file. If there is no receipt (and now with chip and PIN technology this would be less relevant), your credit card company will send you an affidavit to sign and report what happened. Depending on the amount and your relationship with your credit card company, they may or may not release your funds. But it's your right to ask them to do so—especially if you were travelling and had a limit of only $2,000 on your credit card with a fraudulent hold charge of $1,500.

Credit card companies monitor our purchases closely. If something seems unusual, they'll put a freeze on your account. You just need to call them to let them know it was you buying that item outside the price range of your normal spending pattern and they'll release the hold. However, many of us are declined at the point of purchase and don't realize what actually happened until we get home and hear the voice mail message from the credit card company.

Each time you travel, let your credit card company know you'll be away so that (hopefully!) they don't freeze your account while they figure out whether you are actually on a trip.

To help us monitor our own accounts on a frequent basis for signs of fraud, many banks are now offering mobile banking apps for your smartphone or tablet. Some also offer an email service delivered to your smartphone or tablet (there may be a small monthly fee) that notifies you each time your credit/debit card is used. It provides a number to call if you don't recognize this transaction.

Lost or Stolen Cards

If your card has been lost or stolen or the credit card company suspects that your card or account number has been compromised, they may issue you an entirely new card. The wait for the new card is usually just an inconvenience. During the holidays or when travelling, however, this delay could leave you short of funds and unable to move. This is why it's essential to have more than one credit card. You could also demand, especially if it's not your fault, that they courier you a new card the next day. Most credit card companies will do this.

Credit Card Protection

There is a great deal of protection (e.g., extended warranty coverage, car rental insurance, purchase security coverage) that's offered when paying with some credit cards vs. paying with cash or your debit card. Some consumers find that the extra protection is well worth the annual fee that's required. Just remember to always read the fine print. Every credit card offers different rewards, possible protection, annual fees and, of course, interest. For some card users, and particularly those who pay off their balance every month, these perks can be attractive. Please read the fine print of your credit card agreement or go to your bank or credit card company's website for more information about what is covered and what you must do to activate coverage.

Debit Cards

Many of us use a debit card. What I like about this form of payment is that it's like paying with cash in the sense that we're using what we have in our bank account but the amount spent shows up online instantly, so it doesn't delay the pain of the purchase. (With most credit cards, it often takes several days for purchases to show up online). A debit card still doesn't provide the tangibility of cash, but it's a convenient option. Some banks even offer the opportunity to painlessly save as you spend (by transferring a dollar or more on each purchase to your savings account).

The Cost of Using Debit Cards

A debit card allows you to access your bank account from a remote location. So, if you're at the grocery store and don't have enough cash to pay for your groceries, you can use your debit card and the bill is paid instantly, with the money coming directly from your bank account to the grocery store. However, there is a price for this convenience. Banks offer a range of fee packages depending on the type of accounts you have and the number of transactions you make per month. Sixty per cent of Canadians pay $15 or less each month in fees and 31% pay nothing. While $15 per month may not seem expensive, it adds up to $180 per year and $1,800 over a ten-year period—just to take money out of your own account! To take money out of a bank ABM where you do not have an account could cost you between $1 and $5.60 per transaction, and it can cost from $1.50 to $8.60 to use a private operator's ABM.

Think twice before acquiring the habit of using your debit card instead of cash for every purchase, unless you have a no-fee arrangement with your financial institution.

To keep transaction costs down, use only the machines at your own bank and make fewer withdrawals of large enough amounts so that you won't have to make as many withdrawals.

Emailing Money

Sending money by email can be useful for transferring funds after banking hours to someone out of town. Money deposited to an ATM takes several days to clear. But with digital payments, the recipient gets an email within an hour or two. The recipient then logs onto their online bank account and sees that the money has been deposited. You might also email funds where mailing a cheque would be too inconvenient. Most banks charge $1 to email any amount from $10 to a daily maximum of $1,000. (Check with your bank before using this service to determine whether the convenience is worth the cost.)

Other Debt

Using credit cards is certainly not the only way we get ourselves into debt. Let's briefly look at some other types of debt that can get you into trouble if you overspend.

Loans

A loan is an amount of money borrowed from a lender for a much shorter period of time than a mortgage; perhaps for two to five years, although car loans today can extend to seven or eight years. A loan may be secured or unsecured; the latter would have a higher interest rate.

A car loan is secured by the car, which can be repossessed for non-payment; a student loan or a loan to consolidate and pay off other debts is unsecured. Unsecured loans have a more difficult approval process because the lender isn't protected with an asset to go after if the borrower defaults on their payments. Unsecured loans have the penalty of a higher interest rate.

Line of Credit

A line of credit, sometimes referred to as a Personal Line of Credit (PLC), can also be secured or unsecured and the interest rate will reflect that as well. Many Canadians have a secured line of credit on their homes in addition to their mortgage. These are the home-equity lines of credit (HELOCs) mentioned earlier in this chapter. They are secured against the equity, i.e., the portion of the value of the house that is greater than the portion covered by the mortgage. This equity can be composed of two parts: the portion of the original house price paid for through regular or lump-sum mortgage payments and the increase in market value since the purchase.

Suppose you open a $50,000 line of credit to do a house renovation over the next year. You don't take out all the money at once because you don't want to pay interest until you have to pay the contractors. Think of using a line of credit much like you would a credit card: you have a limit that you can use as you please. The interest you pay depends on how much you draw out. The interest rate is significantly lower than that of a credit card.

Consolidation Loan

This type of loan is used to pay off other debts, such as student loans, car loans, credit card balances, etc., that have been acquired separately at different times. The consolidation loan enables you to pay off the individual debts and leaves you with one manageable payment and likely a much lower overall interest rate than you were paying on average for the individual loans.

In theory, a single loan to pay off high-interest debt is a great idea. It's obviously physically and psychologically easier to make just one payment and save on interest. However, it can be a slippery slope into more debt. You have to ask yourself how you got into a position where a consolidation loan was your best option in the first place. Was it because of an illness, disability or simply overspending? Also, a lower payment at lower interest may be enough to create a real temptation to go out and get more credit or overspend again. Some lenders will suspend all or most of your credit while you have a consolidation loan. But sometimes the card companies don't suspend the problem cards after they've been paid off. That paid-off card then becomes a great temptation and, in no time, the card(s) are maxed out again with no second chance of paying off the debt.

Leasing

A lease is a contract for the use of some asset for a fixed price for a fixed period of time. Leases can be for tangible property (usually called a rental agreement) such as a car, heavy equipment, office furniture, office space and a wide range of other items or for intangible property such as computer software.

The decision to lease should be made after you have done the math and decided it would be cheaper to lease than to buy. The key factor is the effect on your cash flow of loan payments to purchase versus lease payments to rent. The advantages of leasing include:

- not having to make a down payment
- lower payments and no risk you will be stuck with an obsolete piece of equipment at the end of the lease
- if you are self-employed, leasing a car may also offer tax advantages if it is used for business purposes.

There are disadvantages to leasing a car:

- You always have a car payment, because as long as you lease you will never really own it.
- There are mileage restrictions and there is a penalty if you go over the allowable limit.
- Insurers may charge higher coverage costs for leased vehicles, so you should check with your insurance company.

Leases can be extremely complex and differ greatly, so always read the fine print and know what you're committing yourself to.

Dangers of Consumer Debt

With today's low interest rates, I hear far too many Canadians referring to lines of credit and mortgages as free money. Just because a line of credit is offered at a going rate of a few percentage points, it doesn't mean one should run out and figure out how to get and spend the money. Yes, of course, there are times when it makes sense to use a line of credit to do a renovation. But, there are more things to consider than just the affordable payment. What happens if (and, more realistically, *when*) rates move up? That payment increases as well. Plus, and here's the important part—*you have to pay back the entire principal*. Many borrowers forget about that and just focus on the interest payment. Sure, $150 a month is affordable, but what about the original $50,000? And what about saving for retirement, paying off other debts and all the other good money management practices we've talked about?

Get Some Credit Even When You Don't Need It

To paraphrase Mark Twain, a banker is there to lend you an umbrella when it's sunny and asks for it back when it begins to rain. Unfortunately, many individuals try to get credit when they're the biggest risk (from the bank's point of view). The time *not* to try to get credit is when you've just changed jobs, gone from steady employment to being self-employed (no fixed pay cheque), are already on maternity leave and more. You should think about your future credit needs when you don't need credit. Setting up a secured line of credit on your home, for example, doesn't cost you anything if you don't need it. Nevertheless, if there is a minor emergency in the future, it's already set up and available without the bank needing to know that your circumstances have changed.

Nonetheless, if you know you're not good with credit and would find the temptation to use it too great, then don't get it. More debt always equals less freedom. If you're uncomfortable using credit or don't handle it well, focus on creating a cash nest-egg instead and keep it safe and liquid.

Say "No" To More Debt

You should just say "No" to:

- more than two (three maximum) credit cards (or any more credit cards if their balances are already at their limit)
- department store credit cards
- financing for furniture
- no payment/no interest offers
- thinking any money is free (no matter how low the interest rate)
- consumer debt: if the only way you can afford a vacation, new clothes, electronics or more (wants, not needs) is to charge it on a credit card without a means for paying it in the near future, save up for it instead—you'll enjoy your purchase much more and reduce your stress in the long-term.

Easy Action Steps

1. Never miss a minimum payment on your credit card and always pay more than asked (even if it's a few dollars).

2. Set up reminders in your calendar for credit card payment due dates, statement dates and other fixed payment dates.

3. Get some cash! Determine a comfortable amount to have with you and in your home and or office in the event of an emergency. A realistic amount should cover you and your family for a long weekend for example.

CHAPTER 7

THE IMPORTANCE OF A GOOD CREDIT SCORE

Money can't buy love, but it improves your bargaining position.

—Christopher Marlowe

The Importance of a Good Credit Score

Are we moving rapidly toward a cashless society? Just over a year ago, the media was reporting on the possibility of doing away with cheques in the near future and now the government is doing away with the penny. What's next?

I fear that we will continue to overspend if money becomes even less tangible. What's worse, some of the credit practices south of the border are starting to spill over up here. Whether you're looking to borrow or not, having a blemished credit score could cost you dearly. In the U.S., landlords and employers can check an individual's credit record. Some provinces in Canada base their insurance rates, in part, on your credit. Many contracts, such as leases, monthly costs for security systems and much more are currently affected by your credit score. Whether this is fair or not, you need to know how to maintain a great score and how to improve a poor one.

Why Credit is Important

Unless you have a very wealthy and generous family, marry rich, win the lottery or know you have a big inheritance coming, you'll need to make use of credit a few, or even many, times over your life. Yes, you can save up for a car, home, university education, starting a business, etc., but most likely you will decide to get what you need more quickly with the help of borrowed funds. The fact that those funds are now being offered at such low rates makes borrowing that much more attractive. However, if you have a poor credit rating, you might have to pay well over standard interest rates and possibly not be approved for borrowing at all (at least until your score improves).

Your score affects more than just future borrowing. Even getting a new cell phone requires a credit check and a decent score. Maintaining an above-average credit score throughout your lifetime is imperative.

Get to Know Your Banker

It's equally important that you build a relationship with your banker. Solidifying your association by having all your bank and investment accounts in one place along with your mortgage or other debts (credit cards, loans, etc.) doesn't guarantee great service and better interest rates in the future, but it does help. Your good credit record, together with the length of time you've been a customer, enables your banker to take that into consideration and go to head office with extra leverage (if needed). Loans are approved by a computer program these days—it's rarely a human or personal process.

Check Your Credit Report Regularly

A frequent personal check of your credit report could ward off fraudulent activity. If you've never seen your own credit report, then please add it to the top of this week's to-do list. After I've explained what's on your report it will become clear why you must check your report regularly. If identity theft has been committed in your name, you'll see irregularities on your report. It still might be too late to prevent the money from being stolen, but it might prevent further damage.

I don't think it's at all fair that we as consumers are so closely controlled in many ways by our score, yet we have to pay to get it. And, if your lender just pulled your credit report for a loan of some type, you can just ask them, right? Wrong. It's illegal for them to share that information. Both Equifax and TransUnion have increased the educational component on their respective websites, but they keep the specific information a secret, such as what actions cause your score to go up or down and by how many points.

Over the years, I've had many volunteers and individuals in desperate need of credit repair that have come to me and allowed me to help them (in many cases significantly increase their score and in a shorter time than one might think) and thus their real-life case studies are the foundation of my knowledge and experience. I've also subjected my own credit score/report as a guinea pig to test what increases or decreases a score and by how much. So, it's hardly science, but what I've discovered over the years will help you know what you need to do to maintain or increase your score. Some tips are obvious and some are completely illogical!

How to Get a Copy of Your Report

Most Canadian lenders use two main credit reporting agencies: Equifax and TransUnion. You can obtain a free credit report from each company as often as you'd like.

First, go to one of their websites and print out a form:

Equifax Canada: www.equifax.ca

TransUnion Canada: www.transunion.ca

Equifax and TransUnion both operate in the U.S., so be sure to check you're on the Canadian sites.

By Mail

Print a form, fill it out and send it by mail. Checking the report you get back is prudent, but this report won't tell you your magic credit score—for that you'll have to pay.

Online Instantly

To get your report online instantly, with or without your score, will cost you.

Equifax: $15.50 for the report alone and $23.95 for the report plus your score and explanation (at the time of printing).

TransUnion: $14.95 for the report alone and $22.90 for the report plus an explanation. For an additional $8 you have the option of having your report sent to you by surface mail.

For $14.95 per month both reporting agencies will provide credit monitoring. If your report is satisfactory and your credit has never been severely damaged and you have never had a problem with fraud, it is unlikely you will need this service. So, checking your report once or twice a year should be sufficient. If you suspect or know there has been fraud, you can have both credit agencies flag your account.

You may find accessing your credit report online a bit difficult the first time. You'll need to have at least 30 minutes (or more) free and a secure place such as your home (and not your office) from which to call Equifax or TransUnion if you get locked out. You'll also want to have the account numbers available for your loans, credit cards, etc.

I asked a good friend of mine, we'll call him Jackson, if he would mind going through the process with me. He was already on Equifax but had never checked his TransUnion score. Since he had recently bought a car and financed it with a loan and taken out a modest line of credit, he was curious to know how his Equifax score reflected this recent activity. Let's follow Jackson's investigation to learn more about the whole process.

Understanding Your Score

Both agencies have proprietary software for calculating their scores, so each score is slightly different. However, the information conveyed by the scores is similar.

The scores work on a range of 300–900 and you want your score to be as high as possible. But don't worry, it doesn't have to be perfect. In fact, recent data showed that fewer than 5% of Canadians have a score of 850 or more. However, more than 57% of Canadians (according to Equifax) have a score of 760 plus. If yours is less than 760, don't worry, but you have some work to do. Even if you have no plans to use credit in the near future, it's still a good idea to have the best credit score possible.

Jackson decided to pay the full amount to get both his report and his score from Equifax so he could compare it with his TransUnion report.

Interestingly, Equifax has a five-category naming protocol for their scoring:

- very poor (300–559)
- poor (560–659)
- fair (660–724)
- good (725–759)
- very good (760+).

TransUnion worded their categories differently and didn't provide specifics on the score for each category. Their scoring is:

- very poor
- poor
- fair
- good
- very good.

Jackson scored 749 with TransUnion and was ranked by them as "fair", but this ranking was "good" with Equifax. In other words, Jackson was ranked only slightly higher than 49.21% of the Canadian population. A few things on Jackson's TransUnion credit report were incorrect. The report listed no late payments when Jackson knew he had made three late payments with one credit card company and one with another. Of the four old addresses listed, two were places where he had never lived. His current address was also wrong.

What Does Your Score Mean For Your Credit Rating?

Your score is an important element when a lender is considering approving you for credit, but it's only one part of the approval process. Your net worth, employment stability, the size of your other debts, length of time in your home and other factors are also considered. Your credit score is only a snapshot of how you've handled your current and past credit.

What Information is on Your Report?

Your report contains the same information you've given your lenders. Information about your debts is supposed to be removed after six years with Equifax, seven years with TransUnion. If you've been bankrupt, that information remains for 10 to 14 years. However, you may see old accounts still on your report, but they should not affect your score past the respective number of years.

The first information you'll see is personal, such as:

- your name
- current and previous addresses
- employment
- SIN
- date of birth.

Again, all of this is information you provided to your last lender.

The next sections itemize each debt:

- loans
- credit cards
- leases
- personal lines of credit and more.

In Canada, a mortgage with one of the big banks is not usually reported on your credit report (although, this is supposed to be changing in the near future with the big banks looking at reporting mortgage activity). Most individuals find this shocking as it's our largest debt. If you've also been exceptional and never missed a mortgage payment, that history isn't reported on your report and doesn't help your score. This section will list:

- creditor's name and phone number
- type of account
  - personal or joint
  - revolving (you can pay it down or run it back up, as with a credit card) or installment (a set amount you pay each month such as a car loan)
  - currently open or closed; if closed, whether payments are up to date
- date the account was opened: having accounts open for long periods of time is good for your score
- date a creditor last reported information
- date you last used the account: if you don't use your account at least every other month, your score can be negatively affected; if you have only a couple of major credit cards, you will use them more frequently than if you have too many
- credit limit
- payment amount
- balance
- past due accounts: balance and past due amounts are some of the most important indicators calculated in your score
- payment history: how many times you've been 30, 60 or 90 days late on a payment; 1 day late on a payment counts as 30; a payment on the 31st day count as 61 days and really hurts your score

(Note: the information in each of the above applies to each creditor on file)

- your credit history and banking information (if any)
- information from public records, such as a bankruptcy, orderly payments of debt, judgments, seizures and more
- collection accounts: usually utilities and cable bills, etc., are not reported on a credit file; however, even if an account has been closed, a small amount could remain owing which could be enough to pull down your score and cause credit to be declined.

Tips for Improving Your Credit Score

- Whenever you close an account of any type, always have a letter mailed or faxed stating that your account has been paid in full and keep it in your files in case of a problem down the line.
- Negotiate: if you owe money to a company and can't pay the entire balance, negotiate. If negotiations don't work, your account will be sent to a collection agency. If something is reported as being in collections but you've actually paid it off, you may need to intervene to get it off your report.
- Get a letter from the creditor that the account has been paid in full. If the item is not off your report in a couple months (I've seen creditors and credit agencies take as long as six months to make changes on reports), you have the documents to show the credit agency it should be removed. (Having something in collections will greatly reduce your credit score.) If, for some reason, you're seeking credit at this time, lenders might be more understanding about your score if you have a letter proving the debt was paid off (your effectiveness with a new creditor will depend to a great extent on how long the debt sat in collections, how large it was, etc.).

Inquiries

Hard Inquiries

When you apply for a loan, lease, credit card, cell phone or anything else requiring credit, the name of the creditor shows up at the end of your credit report (Equifax lists both hard and soft inquiries but TransUnion lists only hard inquiries).

There's a magic "three hits and you're hurt" theory when applying for credit. You don't want to apply for too much credit in a short period of time. Many people do this innocently and don't find out until they're declined on the third credit application.

Consider that you're moving to a new province. You sold your car and, with the amazing dealer financing, you decide to get a new car. Then, you get a line of credit from your bank to do renovations on your new home (you were able to port over your mortgage, so a new application wasn't needed) and then, you go to get a new cell phone plan with a new carrier and you're declined. You can see how easy (and necessary) it can be to apply for too much credit in a short amount of time. Don't think of the credit reporting agencies as thinking, humane, reasoning human beings. No. It's strictly a mathematical formula that says, you must be in trouble if you're "seeking" so much credit in such a short period of time. The reporting agencies don't care what the applications were for, nor can they decipher logic. So, fair or not, do your best to space your credit applications over months—better yet, years.

I mentioned earlier in this book that even if you don't need credit in the future and don't think you need to care about checking your credit, this section could be your tip-off to fraud—that someone may have stolen your identity. If you check your report and see under the hard inquiries a creditor you have never dealt with, you are probably looking at a huge red flag. If that's the case, you'll want to notify both credit reporting agencies immediately; contact the creditor as well and, possibly, the RCMP.

Go to the **Resources** chapter for more information on how to act fast if you think you've been a victim of fraud.

Soft Inquiries

I like the fact that Equifax lists these as well. These inquiries are "peeks" at your credit report without affecting your score. As well, when you check your own score and access your credit report, it shows up in this second category but also does not affect your score. For example, when you sign a credit card application (we all read the details, right?) you're usually agreeing to allow the company to check your credit to see if they'll extend you credit. Further, because revolving credit can be called in by the creditor at any time, they could secretly check to see if they might want to take away your credit extension due to a poor score (which they absolutely can do, and they can demand that you pay your balance off in full). Usually you'll see your credit card company offer you a credit increase just after they've checked your credit report.

Equifax lists their contact information and provides a link for you to download a disputes form or just to update your own information.

How to Keep Your Credit Score Healthy

Your credit score is fluid. It can change every month based on your good, bad and consistent use (or lack thereof) of your credit.

Let's look at what you absolutely must be aware of, especially if you're trying to improve your credit score.

1. **Always make your credit card minimum payment on time—every time!** There's never an exception to this rule. Even 1 day late counts as 30 days late. Each time you have a 30-day hit, it hurts your score and 60- and 90-day delinquencies can dramatically pull down your score. So, never neglect any account. If you find yourself unable to keep up with your minimum payments, see the interview at the end of this chapter and go to the **Resources** chapter for credit counselling resources that can assist you before the problem gets serious. If you, or someone you know needs financial help, encourage them to take care of it immediately because it never, ever gets better on its own—quite the opposite, in fact. If your credit card is with an institution other than your main bank, ensure that you allow at least three-to-five business days for the payment to be processed.

Your Credit Score is Down—The Fine Print Really Is Important!

Chantel was a university student who needed a laptop but didn't have enough cash or enough credit on her credit card to buy one. She went to an office supply store to shop for her laptop and was told by the sales person she could defer the entire payment process for six months, i.e., she wouldn't have to pay either interest or principal for six months if she signed up for their in-store credit. It sounded like the perfect plan. She used her parents' address for the loan application. When a letter arrived at her parents' house confirming the account had been opened and reporting the account balance, her dad promptly gave her a call. She told him not to worry and that she had it under control.

Months went by and every once in a while Chantel's dad would give her a call about the office supply store's letter. Seven months after her purchase, Chantel went to an alternative cell phone carrier to sign up for a new plan and was declined. She was shocked! Her disbelief was understandable because she was never behind in her apartment rent, conscientiously paid her credit card minimum payments on time (they were nearly maxed out, but she was never late) and so on. She dashed home and used her new laptop to pull her credit report and, to her horror, saw that her rating was barely over 500. How could this be? She began to panic. There, in the collections section, sat her office supply account with seven 30-day-late hits, three 60-day-late hits and two 90-day-late hits. A recipe for a ruined credit score.

The next day she marched back to the office store to find out what had happened and tried to talk to the same sales person, but he no longer worked there. Instead, Chantel spoke with customer service and explained that the salesman had led her to believe she wouldn't have to start making payments or be charged interest for six months.

...continued

The truth was that she had accepted a no-interest, *not* a no-payment, option for six months. Did the sales person lie? Maybe. Did Chantel just hear wrong? Perhaps. Nevertheless, whatever had been said, it had been her responsibility to read the fine print before signing her name and she hadn't done so.

Chantel's situation is an example of a very sad but costly innocent mistake that happens all too often. I know the fine print can be daunting at times, but it's your responsibility and right to read it. Take the time to do so. If there is anything you don't understand, don't sign the sales contract until you have cleared it up to your satisfaction.

2. **Always pay more than your minimum monthly balance**
   Your goal should be to pay off your full credit card balance every month. But if you can't, pay as much as you can more than the minimum monthly payment. If you're not convinced what just a dollar a day more could do to impact an ordinary credit card balance (the average Canadian carries $3,700 – $5,000 balance on their credit cards in total), here are some numbers for you to consider.

   Let's assume you have a balance of $4,000 on a department store card that charges 29% annual interest and requires a minimum monthly payment of $120.

   If you make just the minimum payment and never put another new purchase on your card, it will take 28 years and one month to pay off the balance and you will have paid $12,541.19 in interest! Surprised? Since the government forced credit card companies to start reporting how long it will take a consumer to pay off their balance if they only pay their minimum payment, there's really no excuse for us to not be more aware.

If this example sounds similar to your situation, there is one nearly painless solution. Just add a dollar a day to the minimum monthly payment, now totalling $150 a month. The result of such an easy solution? You will now be free of this debt in just three years and six months and pay just $2,233.01 (I still think that's too much) with a savings of nearly 25 years of payments and $10,308 in interest. *For just a dollar more a day!*

3. **Don't go over the limit on your credit cards**
   Never be at your maximum limit. If you find yourself at or very close to your limit because of a one-time major purchase, start paying off every cent you can to create a little cushion. The reason you need to start paying down immediately is that the interest charged on the unpaid balance might be enough to push you over your limit and impair your credit score. Just $20 or $30 is enough to hurt your score. The effect of being over by just $20 or $30 can therefore be much more than just $20 or $30. Some credit cards allow merchants to let you go slightly over your limit to avoid the embarrassment of being declined for a small amount. The amount depends on the customer. What you need to know is that this company has an over-limit fee of $35. If this situation sounds familiar to you or someone you know, you have the right to call the credit card company and ask them to stop allowing this so-called *privilege* on your account.

4. **Limit revolving credit and installment loans**
   It may seem normal to have a balance of around 35%-50% of your total available credit, but ideally you should be under 35%. If you had a credit card limit of $2,500, ideally you shouldn't have a balance of more than $875. As you can imagine, as one approaches or exceeds 90% of their credit limit, the credit agencies see a big red flag.

   When you first take out an installment loan such as a car loan, your score will likely drop and might stay down for a while, as it will appear you've borrowed your credit limit. If you take out a car loan of $30,000, you'll be near your maximum for the first year. There's not really much you can do about that, but, hopefully, if you otherwise have good, long-established credit, your score shouldn't drop too much. However, as long as you always make your payments on time, your score will rebound.

Some Important Credit Don'ts

1. **Don't close bank-issued major credit cards**
   Use them often, but pay the monthly balance off in full. The credit-scoring system will wonder why you closed out a major credit card and become suspicious of your reasons. You're better to keep the card, use it periodically, say every month or two for a small purchase here and there, and then pay the balance off in full each month.

2. **Don't bounce loan payments**
   This is dangerous not only because delinquency will affect your credit score, but also because of those $45 NSF charges.

3. **Don't allow anything to go to collections**
   Negotiate with the company in question. Keep making the payments even if there is a dispute. Just because there's an issue with your car and you want to return it to the dealer, you should continue to make the loan/lease payment and try to recoup costs afterwards. Even if you're in the right at the end of the process, you could dramatically hurt your credit score by not making the payments required under the contract you signed. You're better to try to recover the money later from the company or take the matter to small claims court. By not breaching the contract, you stand on safer legal ground, and will have a better chance of recovering your money through a court-ordered judgment later.

4. **Don't have too much available credit**
   Even if all your revolving credit (usually credit cards) has a zero balance, the system assumes that you *could* go out and max out all your cards tomorrow. I know it sounds bizarre, but the system cannot seem to distinguish between *having* credit and *using* credit. There's no magic number as to how much is too much credit for you, but if you have no late payments, no collections, low-to-zero balances and your score is still unacceptable, it might be because you simply have too much open credit. When you check your credit report, look to see if you have any old accounts (from furniture companies or jewellery stores, perhaps) that you've forgotten about but the system still considers you to have available credit.

5. **Don't open any new department store cards**
   If you currently have more than one, close the ones you rarely use. Fewer cards will be helpful to your score in the long run.

Due Date vs. Statement Date

Some credit cards have the same due date and statement date, but the vast majority don't. The due date is usually indicated very clearly in a box on your credit card statement. That's the date your minimum payment is due. It's also the date by which you need to pay your entire balance if you want to avoid interest payments. The statement date, on the other hand, is the date your statement is generated and the date the credit card company reports to the credit agencies.

Let's suppose your statement date is April 15 (statement dates change—look at the left or right top of your statement for your date). The statement tells you your minimum payment is due on May 8. Around May 15, your next statement will come in saying your next due date is June 8, and so on. Let's also assume you pay your credit card off in full on June 8 and therefore you have no interest charges.

Let's also assume your credit limit is $5,000. You're renovating your home and the hardwood flooring arrives and the cost is $4,900. Your card has a zero balance and you put the flooring on your card. Here's the problem. By chance you put the $4,900 on your card two days before May 15, the statement date. It was the only transaction on the card since you had paid off the entire balance on May 8, the due date. Because the $4,900 went on your card before the statement date, it gets reported to the credit agency. But the credit card company knows you pay your card off in full every month, right? No. Not at all. Your credit card company reports your balance to the credit reporting agency on one date, and on one date only and that's the statement date. Because you were reported near your limit, you could see your score come down.

The moral of this story is: keep track of both the statement and due dates if you're trying to improve your score. Make sure you always pay at least the minimum payment each month and keep your balances as low as possible on statement dates. Remember, since the statement date is usually (but not always) the 15th of the month, you need to keep your balances low from the 14th to the 16th. Put those dates in your calendar as a handy reminder.

Supplementary Cards

Is your credit card really yours? Are you really building credit in your own name? You need to check now.

If you have a supplementary card, it's not your credit account and you're not building credit for yourself. For example, I can get a supplementary card for almost anyone on my credit card account. I can get one for my husband, business partner, assistant, or my niece who's travelling to Europe. Let's say that my husband's only credit card is the one on my account and he has no other debts (or credit) in his name. If I passed away or divorced him, he'd be in deep credit trouble as he would have no credit score.

The card may look as if it's his because he'd have a unique number and name on the card. So how would he know? The monthly statement would be in my name. His purchases (or anyone else's who has a supplementary card on my account) would show up on that statement. However, I'd be responsible for any and all those purchases and to my card's maximum amount. If I'm responsible for all purchases and payments, and applied and approved for the card, I'm the one building credit or being hurt if someone is spending at my credit limit.

Many couples operate with one credit card account for so many years and they lose track of whose account it really is and never think of this being an issue. If you currently have only a supplementary credit card, get one in your own name! It doesn't have to be a card with a large limit and you might consider one with no annual fee or rewards. But without it you can't build your personal credit.

Protect Your Identity

According to the Canadian Anti-Fraud Centre, there were 4,606 reported cases of identity theft in Canada in 2011 and 17,002 cases of identity fraud for a total loss of $13.2 million. The Centre estimates that these statistics represent less than 5% of the total number of victims overall.

In January 2010, Canada gained a new law which created three new offences under the *Criminal Code* with regard to identity theft:

- obtaining and possessing identity information with the intention of using it deceptively, dishonestly or fraudulently
- trafficking in identity information for criminal purposes
- possessing or trafficking in government-issued identity documents.

Identity thieves are looking for:

- full name
- date of birth
- Social Insurance Numbers
- full address
- mother's maiden name
- username and password for online services
- driver's licence number
- personal identification numbers (PIN)
- credit card information (numbers, expiry dates and the last three digits printed on the signature panel)
- bank account numbers
- signature
- passport number

Dos and Don'ts to Help Protect Yourself

Here are a few things you can do to keep yourself safe. Prevention is key—it's a great deal easier to do the small things to secure your identity than to deal with the possible devastation later.

1. **Don't carry more information than you need.**
   Carry only your driver's licence, one credit and debit card and some cash. Always keep your passport at home (in a safe, if possible) along with your SIN card.

2. **Don't show your ID for purchases with your credit card.**
   (This is happening much less with the chip and PIN technology). If a merchant needs to see your signature and you show your driver's licence, for example, and they have a hidden camera, they would then have your date of birth, full name, full address and driver's licence number. That gives a would-be thief a great deal of information to commit a crime in your name. However, if you are travelling in the U.S., they may insist on other ID. I suggest you use white-out tape to cover all your information except for your name and signature.

3. **Do check your credit score often.**

4. **Do make a list of bills and check their arrival dates.**
   If you don't receive a bill by the expected date, call the creditor. Bills stolen from your mailbox can give important account and personal information that can be used to defraud you.

5. **Do install a mail slot if possible.**
   Identity theieves can steal your mail from an unlocked mailbox.

6. **Don't make calls to your bank or credit card company that require you to say out loud your secret password in front of anyone.**
   Don't state it in front of a partner, friend, co-worker—anyone. Sadly, a great deal of fraud is committed by people close enough to us to be trusted.

7. **Do call your bank and credit card companies and add a second secret password to your account.**
   Be sure you remember this one. (Default is usually our mother's maiden name, which is pretty easy to find out).

8. **Do shred everything with even the slightest bit of personal information on it.**

9. **Don't *ever* respond to an email asking you for any personal or financial information or to change any password, update information or more (unless you initiated a change).**
   Your bank would never send you an email asking for any personal information (and scammers are getting so good at fooling even the brightest computer user). When in doubt, call the company in question or go directly to their website—never use the link that an email phisher has included.

For more specific information on protecting yourself from identity theft, go to **www.financialdecisionsmatter.com** for suggestions from the Privacy Commissioner of Canada.

Conversation with Laurie Campbell (CEO, Credit Canada Debt Solutions)

Q: What are the top warning signs that someone is in over their head financially and should call up a credit counsellor?

A: The top three warning signs are:

1. Borrowing from one credit card or line of credit to pay the other.
2. Relying on credit for day-to-day purchases.
3. Stressed out about finances—from not being able to sleep to feeling ill—if you're worried that you won't have a roof over your head next month, it's time to take some action.

Q: What does a credit counselling company offer?

A: First, ensure you're dealing with a non-profit credit counselling company. They offer services such as budgeting assistance, how to manage your debt, debt resolution and all the steps along the way. And you don't need to be in severe debt. You might contact a credit counsellor to simply set you on the right financial path even if you're not in dire need.

Credit counsellors understand that feeling overwhelmed by debt can happen to anyone. They can provide comfort to the struggling individual and see new angles. Also confirm that your credit counsellor is certified. Services are completely confidential, non-judgmental and come with support, expertise, and an in-depth look at your situation and more.

Your first consultation is extensive and absolutely free. There may be fees later, depending on the debt resolution path. However, that first appointment, generally an hour-and-a-half, will provide the individual with a comprehensive look at their situation with a certified counsellor. They can then determine the right path for you.

Q: What should you look out for?

A: Do your research and shop around. Find a non-profit credit counselling company, ask if their counsellors are certified, accredited and belong to an association, and are licensed in the province in which they operate.

Be cautious of any company that charges large fees up-front, makes things more confusing or vague, encourages no conversation or action with your creditors and, lastly, sounds too good to be true.

Financial troubles aren't just stressful, they can be shameful. But it doesn't have to be that way. You can talk on the phone with someone who can help and who can offer concrete advice for no initial charge. Time is never a friend in a financial time of need and debts never go away or resolve themselves. If you feel that any of the three warning signs apply to you, get help today (see the **Resources** chapter for a listing of non-profit credit counsellors in Canada).

www.creditcanada.com

Easy Action Steps

1. Even if you're not concerned about your score, you should check your credit report at least once or twice a year to ensure the information is correct and your identity hasn't been used to apply for credit for someone else.
2. When you close an account, ensure that you get a letter from the creditor stating the account is closed and it has a zero balance.
3. Check that you're actually building credit in your own name. If you're unsure if you have a supplementary card, call up the credit card company or check the monthly statement.

CHAPTER 8

INVESTMENTS FOR TODAY AND FOR YOUR FUTURE

The mint makes it first,
it's up to you to make it last.

—Evan Esar

Investments for Today and for Your Future

The world of investing is vast and can be complex; so this book is intended as a brief introduction. I'll do my best to clearly explain the basics of investing without going into too much detail. If some concepts still aren't as clear as you'd like when you finish reading this chapter, please don't despair; it becomes much easier once you actually start investing your own money. Think of it as taking a course about the history of Europe and then actually going there to see the historic sites; nothing can really compare with experiencing things first hand, but this is a good place to start.

I hope this chapter will inspire you to read more in the near future.

Investing 101

A tax shelter is a place where you can put your money (i.e., invest your money) to defer or avoid paying tax, either in the form of income tax or capital gains tax. However, tax shelters are not in themselves investments; they are merely the place where you keep your investments in much the same way you keep your car in a garage. The car is the investment, the garage is the tax shelter.

There are three main kinds of investments:

1. Cash or cash equivalents, i.e., assets that can be turned into cash within three months
2. Fixed-income
3. Equity.

Cash and Cash Equivalents

Cash is cash and cash equivalents are marketable securities that can be turned into cash in fewer than three months.

Savings Accounts

These are bank accounts which may or may not pay much interest. In the past, investors were treated to double-digit interest payments on savings accounts, so they seemed to be a good investment. However, inflation was also high and, when interest rates are high, inflation takes a bite out of that interest. Today, inflation is extremely low, so interest rates are low as well. Rates can vary quite a bit so it's good to shop around.

Term Deposits

A term deposit is a loan to a financial institution (e.g., $1,000) for a fixed period of anywhere from a month to less than a year. The longer the term, the higher the interest rate. The money can only be withdrawn at the end of the term. If it is withdrawn before that time there is usually a penalty. The penalty is compensation to the bank for at least some of the interest lost because of your early withdrawal.

The lower the risk of the investment, the lower the interest paid.

Fixed Income

This is where you lend your money for longer periods of time than a year. The borrower (the financial institution) makes interest payments to you and returns principal on a pre-established (fixed) schedule.

Guaranteed Investment Certificates (GICs)

GICs are usually purchased at your local bank or credit union. Issuers of GICs guarantee to pay you interest and repay your principal at the end of a fixed period of time, usually ranging from one to five years. The longer that you allow the bank to hold onto your money (the term to maturity, i.e., when you get your money back from them) the greater the accumulated interest that you'll be paid on your investment. GICs are based on current interest rates, which are currently fairly low. However, your principal (the original amount you gave/lent the bank) is guaranteed, as is your interest rate. You're the lender and you have to figure out what's best for your situation (i.e., Should I tie up my money for a long time?) and also, where are interest rates going? With your mortgage, you worry about locking in to a fixed rate and then the rates could drop. With a GIC, you'd be concerned about the opposite; locking in to a rate and then the rates could go up.

Make sure your financial institution is a CDIC member or insured under a provincial plan

Some investments are insured up to $100,000 with the Canada Deposit Insurance Corporation (CDIC). The CDIC was established to protect deposits held by member financial institutions in case an institution fails. There is no need to sign up or pay a premium because the member institutions pay to insure their own depositors against losses. However, not all financial institutions are members of the CDIC.

For a complete list of members, visit the CDIC website (**www.cdic.ca**) and click on "Where Are My Savings Insured by CDIC". Only deposits at member institutions are insured.

Bonds

Bonds are loans to governments and corporations and are usually in units of $1,000. Unlike Term Deposits and GICs, bonds trade on the open market.

These can be very complex investments, even though they can be a low to moderate risk. You need to decide for how long you're going to lock in, for example, 10 to 30 years. The type of bond you buy (a Government of Canada bond, a provincial or municipal bond or even a corporate bond), will determine the interest rate you get. Generally, the higher the interest rate, the higher the risk.

A bond issued by a government, such as a 10-year Government of Canada bond, is usually considered to be low risk because the federal government has the taxing power to raise the money to repay the loan. A corporation, on the other hand, could run into trouble and be unable either to pay the interest or repay the principal. If there is any risk of such failure, the borrower (the corporation) will have to pay a higher interest rate to borrow the money from you.

The lower the risk of the investment, the lower the interest that is paid. The interest rate for bonds is quite low, but higher than a GIC. However, a bond can be bought and sold on a bond market before it matures, unlike most simple GICs which can't be cashed before maturity.

Bond Prices

If a $1,000 bond is issued at 5% for 10 years, the purchaser receives $50 every year for 10 years, at which time the issuer will repay the $1,000. If interest rates move up to 5.5% for bonds of comparable quality, the price of the bond on the market will decline to $900 because anyone willing to buy the bond now wants 5.5% on their money instead of only 5%. Since the $50 payment is fixed, the bond price has to decline to $900 to give the new purchaser a 5.5% yield when getting only $50.

If interest rates go up, bond prices go down; if interest rates go down, bond prices go up.

Equity

Equity ownership is expressed in units of ownership called stocks (American-English) or shares (Canadian-English). The need for buyers and sellers to interact with each other on short notice led to the creation of stock exchanges.

If a company needs to raise large amounts of capital, it usually offers its shares or debt to the general public. In order to do this, the company has to register with one of the provincial securities commissions in Canada. The securities commissions require companies to provide sufficient basic financial information so that members of the public can make an informed decision about whether or not to buy the securities. The securities commissions also require existing issuers to file financial information quarterly and annually.

However, because shares are listed on a major exchange it does not mean they are without risk. The stock exchanges and securities commissions do not monitor the risk involved in buying a company's shares.

Types of Shares

There are two primary classes of shares: preferred and common.

Preferred

Preferred shares are much like bonds: they generally have a fixed dividend and their market price moves with interest rates, i.e., upward when rates decline and downward when rates go up. Preferred dividends are also eligible for the dividend tax credit. If the company goes into bankruptcy, preferred shareholders stand after bondholders and before common shareholders for the distribution of the proceeds of any sale of company assets.

Common

Common shares tend to move in relation to the outlook for company earnings. This relation is usually expressed as the "price earnings multiple". For example, a company expected to earn $2 per share in the current fiscal year might see the market price of its stock trading at $40 (or 20 times earnings). This would mean that investors are expecting a strong performance from the company. The multiple might be quite a bit higher for a company whose earnings growth rate is expected to be substantially above average, or might be lower for a company whose earnings are stable but more slow-growing.

If the company does well or the market expects it to do well, the share price will go up. And the reverse will also happen. Some shares can be conservative and grow steadily; others can be an extremely high risk. There are no guarantees when investing in shares; you can make a huge return or you could lose some or all of your investment. You share in the company's success or failure. However, the opportunity for growth can be a huge lure, but most definitely shares are not for the faint of heart. You should also be aware that, in theory, common shares tend to move in relation to the outlook for company earnings, but shares can also move based on other factors (such as speculative information) and this can create "bubbles" that burst.

Dividend Reinvestment Plans [DRIPs]

Many major Canadian companies have DRIPs where, instead of you taking the quarterly dividend in cash, the plan purchases additional shares for you (often at a discount to the market price). This continues every quarter and the effect is the same as compounding interest. The plan is a form of automatic savings for you every quarter. Dividend increases provide additional money, so the rate of return can be quite significant.

Portfolio Management

Portfolio management begins with the establishment of your goals. What do you want the portfolio to do:

- Provide for retirement 35 years down the road through an RRSP?
- Educate your children through an RESP?
- Establish an emergency fund in case of a crisis through a TFSA?

Your goal, the length of time you have to achieve that goal, the kind of risk you can tolerate, plus the changing risk-reward ratio of the various asset markets through the years will all have to be taken into consideration when you decide on what you need to own.

Asset Allocation

If you've done any investing or studied the subject, you will have come across the term "asset allocation". It may sound a bit complex, but it just refers to diversification. Essentially, there are three main assets: cash, fixed income and equity (shares). The percentage of each that you should have invested depends not on the current markets or interest rates but on one, or a combination, of these factors:

- How much do you have to invest?
- How many years is it until you will need your funds?
- How much risk or volatility can you handle in your portfolio?
- What is your net worth?
- What is your level of financial education?

A rule of thumb for a portfolio is 100 minus your age for your percentage in equities, with the remainder being divided among bonds and cash.

A young person can tolerate a higher proportion of equities in their portfolio for two reasons: first, because they want to benefit from the long-term capital growth and dividend increases and, second, because they have the earning power to replace any losses. As a person approaches retirement, there is less tolerance of risk; the proportion of fixed-income investments should increase.

Generally, there will be a place for some equities because of the need for dividend growth and capital gains to offset the erosion of buying power caused by inflation. Cash management will also always be an important part of any portfolio performance since the proceeds of sales and cash deposits kept must continue to earn interest.

Mutual Funds

During workshops, I'll ask attendees if mutual funds are risky or safe and if they are a good investment or a bad one. As you can imagine, I get every possible answer—and every possible answer is correct!

You can usually get into a fund for $500, or even as little as $25 per month (each mutual fund has a minimum initial investment amount and a monthly investment amount), which you cannot do if you are buying shares or bonds on the open market. Also, if you wanted to save monthly, you can't do that with T-bills, bonds or even shares, but you can with mutual funds.

The four most popular types of mutual funds are:

1. Money market funds
2. Bond funds
3. Equity funds
4. Balanced funds.

Money Market Funds

As the name suggests, these funds invest in investments that repay principal in less than a year. Fund managers buy and sell these investments to maximize the return on the fund. A money market fund can be a good place to park your money for short periods.

Bond Funds

These funds invest in debt with maturities greater than a year. Bond fund managers also try to maximize the fund's rate of return by trading a portfolio of fixed-income investments of varying maturities and yields by including both government and corporate bonds.

Equity Funds

There is an enormous variety of these funds. They can specialize in certain industries or countries, be high risk or conservative. They can even focus on providing high-yielding dividend income. International funds focus on foreign markets with their associated risks of political instability and adverse movements in exchange rates.

Balanced Funds

This type of fund has a diversified portfolio including cash, fixed income and equity investments in one fund and it focuses on moderate risk and moderate returns.

Advantages of Mutual Funds

- Mutual funds sell units of the fund rather than shares and bonds directly. When you buy a unit, you contribute to a pool of money used by fund managers to purchase the shares and bonds that make up the fund's portfolio. So, for a small outlay, you can own a piece of a highly diversified investment.
- Mutual funds are usually managed by experienced professionals who spend 100% of their career monitoring and educating themselves about all investment matters.
- Many fund companies with "families" of funds allow you to move from one fund to the other without paying a commission.

For a minimum investment of only $500 you can get exposure to shares you couldn't possibly purchase on your own for the same amount of money.

Disadvantages of Mutual Funds

- Mutual funds have a similar risk to any other kind of investment. You can lose your investment just as easily in a mutual fund as you can if you purchased shares, bonds, etc., outside the fund.
- The most common criticisms of mutual funds are that they charge too much in commissions and management fees and they often do not outperform the common measures of performance such as the S&P/TSX Composite Index.

High Cost

Commissions

Before you buy a fund you should understand how the commission structure works. There are several types:

- Front-end load funds charge a purchase commission which may be negotiable and vary from one mutual fund company to another (the commissions charged are usually between 2% and 5%). No fees are charged when you sell the fund.
- Back-end loads charge a commission only when you sell and are not negotiable. You are normally not charged a back-end load to move from one fund to another within the fund company's "family" of funds. You pay when you leave the family. You usually have to stay with the family of funds for five to seven years before you can sell without paying any commission. If you sell early, then you pay a commission based on how many years you have been invested in the fund—the more years invested, the smaller the commission.
- Some fund companies have no-load funds.

These commissions may also pay, in part, for the advice that you receive from your financial advisor, therefore your advisor may be motivated to sell you a particular fund. Before buying any fund, it is a good idea to ask your advisor how they are compensated.

Management Expense Ratio (MER)

The Management Expense Ratio (MER) is the percentage of a fund's annual average assets taken by the fund management company to pay for administrative costs such as bookkeeping, research, legal and custodial services as well as the salaries of managers. The MER can range from less than 1% for some money market funds to almost 3% for equity funds. Canadian MERs have been criticized because they're some of the highest of any country surveyed by Morningstar surveys.[2]

2 Morningstar, Inc. is a Chicago-based provider of investment information to individuals, financial advisors and institutions in 27 countries around the world. Among its services are performance surveys of mutual funds.

Since the return you earn on your investment is calculated after the deduction of the MER, your actual return is substantially less than the total return of the fund. This can be a significant factor affecting the growth of your savings in times of low returns (such as we are living in now). While funds with high MERs may be worth it because of the professional managers they use, it means that those same managers need to work that much harder to earn you a decent rate of return.

Shop around and compare fees for similar funds in other fund families to ensure the fees you could be charged are fair and reasonable.

Poor Performance

Another major criticism of mutual funds is that they generally don't outperform the main indices that are usually taken as proxies for the market as a whole. For example, the S&P/TSX Composite Index is usually taken to represent Canadian shares; the Dow Jones Industrial Average and S&P 500 are taken to represent the U.S. market. The annual percentage gains and losses of these indices plus the indices on other major overseas markets are taken to be the standards against which individual portfolio performances are measured. The test is whether the choices of a highly paid fund manager can beat the performance of a collection of shares listed on a stock exchange.

If XYZ Canadian Equity earned a total return of 8% last year and the MER was 2%, you as the investor would have received a net return of 6%. However, if your mutual fund lost money, you would still be charged the 2% MER, thus increasing your loss. These low numbers might not sound like much, but just one percentage point difference in the MER of a mutual fund (e.g., from 2% to 3%) could mean a significant difference over years of investing (and this is in addition to a front-end or back-end load). Costs like that could break a person's retirement!

Index Funds and Exchange Traded Funds

For many people the solution to this under-performance problem has been to buy index funds or Exchange Traded Funds (ETFs), which track the return of a major index (such as the S&P/TSX Composite Index). Today, there are many index funds and ETFs on the market that track many different indices. You can buy one that tracks a Canadian equity index, a Canadian bond index, a

U.S. equity index, international equity index, and more. Because index funds and ETFs simply mirror how the index performs, there's no real management involved. As a result, the MERs are often less than 1%.

Index funds and ETFs are similar in concept because they both track an index, but there are some differences.

Index Funds

- Trade like a mutual fund because you can only purchase them at the end of each day when the price is determined.
- May need to pay a commission similar to mutual funds but many are no-load.
- MERs are much lower than most mutual funds, but tend to be higher than the MERs for ETFs.

ETFs

- Trade like shares because you can purchase them throughout the trading day and have the ability to specify the price at which you are willing to buy or sell.
- You pay a commission every time you buy or sell.
- MERs tend to be lower than index funds.

An equity mutual fund management team needs to make great picks from accurate research and forecasts in order to beat the market as measured by the indices. But even if they come close or do better than the market in a given year, because the MER with an actively managed fund is substantially higher than that of an index fund or ETF, mutual fund managers have to do much better than the market and do it every year. Because many mutual funds underperform their benchmark indices, a number of financial experts suggest that an index fund or ETF might be a better option for some investors.

Easy Action Steps

1. Take the time to truly understand your financial goals before investing or making changes to your investments. Just because the markets change, your portfolio shouldn't, unless your situation has changed (e.g., marriage, divorce, death, job loss).

2. Take a good look at the risk level of your investments. Most of us think we can handle more risk when markets are doing well but, when markets decline, too many sell and realize a crushing loss. You're better off being in a safer investment if it will help you sleep at night.

3. Make a point of finding out what your professional is charging you. If they're evasive or make you feel uncomfortable, shop around for a second or third opinion.

CHAPTER 9

TAX SHELTERS TO HELP YOU SAVE MONEY AND DEFER TAXES

A penny here, and a dollar there,
placed at interest, goes on accumulating,
and in this way the desired result is attained.
It requires some training, perhaps, to accomplish
this economy, but when once used to it, you will find
there is more satisfaction in rational saving
than in irrational spending.
—P. T. Barnum

Tax Shelters to Help You Save Money and Defer Taxes

When I give talks, I often ask my Canadian audiences the question: Do you think an RRSP is an investment? Most Canadians (and that includes those who *have* RRSPs) answer with a resounding, Yes!

The answer is No. This chapter will explain why RRSPs and other similar vehicles are not investments, but actually tax shelters, and will show how you can use them to save money and defer taxes.

What is a Tax Shelter?

A tax shelter is a place you can put your money (i.e., invest your money) to defer or avoid paying income tax. Shelters are not in themselves investments; they are merely the place where you keep your investments in much the same way you keep your car in a garage. (We introduced this concept in **Chapter 8, Investments**: the car is the investment, the garage is the tax shelter.)

Since The Plan (see **Chapter 2**) requires you to pay yourself first, we have to start with what you should do with those savings. In **Chapter 8** we discussed the various types of investments available to you for your savings, so let's identify the main tax shelters for these investments:

- **RRSP**—Registered Retirement Savings Plan
- **RRIF**—Registered Retirement Income Fund
- **RESP**—Registered Education Savings Plan
- **TFSA**—Tax Free Savings Account
- **RDSP**—Registered Disability Saving Plan

I want you to think of all these tax shelters as empty garages. You still need to put cars in your garages.

Remember the different investment choices we covered in the last chapter? If any of those investments (let's pretend they're cars) are purchased within a garage, they are subject to favourable tax treatments. That's really the basis of this chapter. If your investments (cars) are purchased on their own outside a tax shelter (garage), their taxation is different than if they were in a tax shelter (one of the garages).

You can buy bonds, T-bills, GICs, stocks, mutual funds, etc., outside of a garage—this is called a non-registered account. It means that there isn't a shelter because they're not in a registered plan. Or, in other words, the income generated within the account is taxable—you pay tax on them each year or when you sell them. Being "registered" just means that it is a type of account that is recognized by the Canada Revenue Agency to defer or avoid paying income tax. That's why RRSPs, RRIFs, RESP and RDSP all start with "Registered". Even though TFSAs don't include "Registered", you should think of a TFSA as if it were a Registered Tax-Free Savings Plan.

Taxation of Income in Non-Registered Accounts

Interest
Interest is fully taxable.

Capital gains
Capital gains get preferential treatment and are only 50% taxable.

Dividends
Dividends also get preferential treatment as you receive a dividend tax credit that aims to offset the tax already paid by the corporation on the earnings being paid to you.

Tax shelters (RRSP, RRIF, RESP, TFSA and RDSP) are not investments; they're simply empty garages that need to be filled with cars—your investments. Although the tax treatment of each tax shelter and the rules governing it is different, you can put essentially the same investments into each of them. With all of the tax shelters you can invest in shares, bonds, GICs, T-bills, mutual funds, EFTs, etc., so you can usually buy almost any major investment within your RRSP, RRIF, RESP, TFSA and RDSP.

Think of tax shelters as garages. RRSPs, RRIFs, RESPs, TFSAs and RDSPs are empty garages. Investments are the cars you put in the garage.

RRSPs

An RRSP is the most common and well-known tax shelter. The Registered Retirement Savings Plan was introduced to give Canadians who don't have a company pension plan the opportunity to save for retirement through tax-deductible contributions to a tax-sheltered fund.

RRSP Highlights

- your investments grow tax-deferred
- your contributions are tax-deductible to help reduce your income taxes
- you may contribute up to 18% of your earned income each year (subject to limits) plus any "contribution room" not used in prior years
- withdrawals are taxable
- your final contribution will be in the year you turn 71
- may be transferred to your spouse upon death with no tax consequences.

Tax-Deferral

When you invest in an RRSP, your investments grow tax deferred and you don't pay tax on them until you take them out or pass away. Because they grow tax deferred, no tax is owing on any income you generate each year.

Remember, tax deferral doesn't mean tax free. The government will want to collect their tax from you eventually. The RRSP holder is forced to make a change at age 71 (we'll cover RRIFs and retirement options later). If an RRSP holder passes away, all of their RRSP can transfer tax free to a spouse. But if they don't want to transfer their plan to a spouse or one doesn't exist, the plan is totally taxable in the year of their death.

Making Contributions

The amount you can contribute to your RRSP each year is determined by the CRA and is based on your gross income for the previous year. You can contribute up to 18% of earned income from the previous year (to a maximum of $22,970 in 2012 and $23,820 in 2013), minus any adjustments made for contributions you made to an employer's pension plan—the blue Notice of Assessment you get every year after filing your taxes tells you how much you're able to contribute for the following year.

To make your contribution count for a particular tax year, you must make your contribution by March 1st (February 29th in leap years) of the following year. For example, you have until March 1, 2013 to make that contribution count for 2012 when you're filing your 2012 taxes. If you don't fully use your contribution limit each year, you can carry forward that amount indefinitely for use in a future year. Let's say that your 2011 Notice of Assessment stated that your limit for 2012 was $8,640, but you only contributed $4,000 towards your RRSP in 2012. Assuming you had the same income as 2011, you could contribute another $8,640 plus the $4,640 that you didn't use last year. You are allowed a lifetime over-contribution of $2,000. However, be sure not to exceed that amount because if you do, you'll be hit with penalties and a severe headache from the paperwork, so you'll want to make sure you avoided this at all costs!

Contribution Strategies

- If you don't have the cash saved up for your RRSP contribution, you may be eligible for an RRSP loan. Financial institutions offer short-term loans to allow you to make your contribution in time for the March 1st deadline which you can repay when you receive your income tax refund later that year.
- Rather than borrowing the money for your annual contribution, a better method is to set up a monthly investment plan, otherwise known as "paying yourself first". Arrange with your bank to use their pre-authorized transfer service to transfer money from your bank account into your RRSP. The money can be accumulated there, taking advantage of compounding returns and you can choose where it will be invested later. Plus, it's a lot easier for most people to treat this transfer as a recurring payment than to scramble to find a larger lump sum before the end of the following February. Most people don't miss money that they never see!
- In addition to getting an RRSP for yourself, you can create one for your spouse or common-law partner in their name to take advantage of income splitting. This is a particularly useful strategy if your spouse or partner has a lower income than you. If your spouse or partner is in a lower tax bracket than you are at retirement, they will pay less tax than you would if all the money had been in your RRSP.

  You can contribute part of your eligible amount to their RRSP account while you get to deduct the amount from taxable income. Note that, while you made the contributions to their account, the money belongs to them so you have no control over the activity in their RRSPs.

Withdrawals

While you can take funds out of your RRSP at any time, there are consequences. Any funds you take out from your RRSP are fully taxed and form part of your income. Another consequence is that you won't be able to recontribute the amount you withdrew back into your RRSP.

Before investing in an RRSP, ensure the funds won't be needed until retirement. If an emergency occurs, consider drawing funds from your savings account or consider using a personal line of credit. Two exceptions from the above rules apply to first-time home buyers and those planning to head back to school.

Lifelong Learning Plan

- You or your spouse or common-law partner can withdraw up to $10,000 in one year from your RRSPs up to a total of $20,000 over four years to fund education for yourselves or each other only. You do not have to include these amounts in your income and your financial institution will not withhold any income tax.
- You have to repay the withdrawn money within 10 years.

Home Buyers' Plan

- Each of you, your spouse or your common-law partner, can withdraw up to $25,000 per year from your own plan to buy or build a home (provided you are first-time buyers).
- You can also withdraw money to buy or build a house for a related person with a disability.
- The withdrawn money is not included in your taxable income in the year withdrawn.
- You must repay something every year until the full amount is repaid within 15 years.

Filing Your Income Taxes

As noted earlier, the Notice of Assessment that you received from filing the previous year's tax return will let you know the maximum amount that you can contribute to your RRSP for the current tax year. Once you make your contributions, you'll get a tax receipt at the end of the year so that you can calculate your income taxes.

While you are allowed to contribute up to the maximum stated on your Notice of Assessment, you don't necessarily need to include the RRSP deduction on that year's income tax return. If you have low income but you've made a contribution, it may be beneficial for you to defer using the deduction if you believe that your income will increase in the coming years. By deferring the deduction to a higher income year, you would get a bigger benefit from using that deduction, and your contribution grows on a tax-deferred basis in the meantime!

Sometimes investors choose not to contribute to their RRSPs in low-income-earning years. Instead they carry their contribution amount forward to use it in a higher-income year.

When Not to Invest in an RRSP

- You'll need the money in the near future
- You're using it for emergency savings
- You are in a low-income tax bracket
- You believe you might have high income in your retirement years. At retirement, your entire retirement income including a pension (if one exists), your spouse's pension, Canada Pension Plan (CPP) payments and Old Age Security (OAS), any income from investments held outside a tax shelter, plus a forced RRIF withdrawal could move you into a higher tax bracket, thereby causing the government to reduce or even eliminate your OAS.

RRSP vs. Non-RRSP Savings

Inside a Tax Shelter or Outside?

The following case shows the advantage of holding the same investments in an RRSP compared with holding them outside and unsheltered in a non-registered portfolio.

Kristie earns $81,000 and lives in Ontario, so her marginal tax bracket is 39.41% (the combined federal and provincial tax she must pay). Given that all factors are equal, she's wondering what the difference will be by investing in an RRSP vs. a Non-registered account.

- She has 25 years until retirement and will contribute $500 a month
- Assume both the RRSP and non-registered accounts grow by 5% annually
- She's starting with $20,000 in both scenarios.

At the end of 25 years, she'd have $361,845 saved in an RRSP and, with the identical criteria, would have only $265,384 in a non-registered account. All things being equal, if she invested in an RRSP, she'd have $96,460 more than if she invested outside of a garage. However, Kristie would still need to pay tax as the funds are withdrawn from her RRSP/ RRIF during her retirement.

RRIFs

RRIF Highlights

- created by rolling over your RRSP no later than December 31st of the year you turn 71
- withdraw a minimum amount annually according to an age-based percentage schedule
- withdrawals subject to tax (based on your marginal tax bracket)
- cannot make new contributions
- assets which remain in the plan continue to grow tax deferred.

Converting Your RRSP into a RRIF

A RRSP holder can convert to a RRIF at any age but, by December 31st of the year in which you turn 71, you must have opened a RRIF and moved your RRSP investments into it. In other words, you have to get a new garage for your car and, all those cars that are in the RRSP, they simply roll over untouched to the new garage or tax shelter called the RRIF. As with the RRSP, the funds that aren't withdrawn from your RRIF continue to grow tax deferred.

This is the CRA's way of forcing you to convert your savings into taxable income. This move is made by simply filling out a form at your financial institution. There is no need to make any changes to your RRSP in anticipation of the move; the creation of the RRIF is purely administrative.

You start to receive income from the RRIF in the year after you set it up. This is when the government starts to try to recover some of the taxes they let you defer as you built your RRSP. You must take out a minimum payment every year from your RRIF determined by a government calculation, however, you can take out more any time. But all withdrawals are taxable. Your

By December 31st of the year in which you turn 71, you must have opened a RRIF and moved your RRSP investments into it. The funds that aren't withdrawn from your RRIF continue to grow tax deferred.

financial institution will set up a schedule based on your age to withdraw a certain percentage of your money annually to comply with the requirements of the CRA.

Using Age to Your Advantage

You can also elect to base the payment schedule on the age of your spouse or common-law partner. If that person is significantly younger, the minimum amount you have to withdraw is significantly less.

Resheltering Can Save Taxes

Withdrawing the money does not mean you have to spend it; all you have to do is report it as taxable income. You could reinvest up to $5,000 of it in a TFSA every year to reshelter it, or invest it elsewhere. You just cannot put any new money into your RRIF. The money remaining in the RRIF continues to be tax sheltered.

Withdrawals Can Affect Your OAS

In 2012, if you are 65 or over and your total income is $69,562 or more you will have to pay back a portion of your OAS. If your total income is $112,772 you will have to return all of it. Advanced planning with a financial planner early on is recommended to save you tax now and later.

RESPs

RESP Highlights

- designed for families to save for their children's post-secondary needs
- total contribution maximum is $50,000 per beneficiary (child)
- the government will match 20% of your contribution up to $7,200
- contributions are not tax deductible, but investments in the plan grow tax deferred
- withdrawals by the beneficiary are taxable (but the taxes paid are likely to be little or nil)
- contributions are returned tax free if the proposed beneficiary does not go on to post-secondary education.

There are three types of RESPs:

- **Family:** for any child related to you, such as your own children, grandchildren, adopted children, brothers and sisters.
- **Individual:** for one person of any age, even an adult, and not necessarily related to you.
- **Group:**
  - for one child not necessarily related to you
  - contributions are combined with those of other subscribers (contributors).

The RESP can be used to finance education at a college or university in Canada or abroad. It can also be used to pay for skills development in non-credit courses at institutions recognized by Human Resources and Skills Development Canada. See the **Resources** chapter for useful links.

Family RESPs

The usual type of RESP is the family plan, which can be opened by a parent, grandparent or other eligible subscriber for a child or children of the extended family. Not only can the family members contribute, but the children who will be future beneficiaries can contribute to their own plans. RESPs can be opened at most financial institutions. RESPs are also available from group plan dealers and certified financial planners. Contributions to any form of RESP are *not* tax deductible to the subscriber. If for some reason the money is never paid out to the beneficiary, the RESP provider (usually financial institutions) will return the contributions and they will *not* have to be included in the income of the contributor at that time. Any interest, dividends or capital gains earned on the contributions will be subject to tax. Be wary of RESPs that have excessive fees. Most reputable financial institutions will offer plans with very moderate fees. *Be sure to check this out before you sign anything.* (For more information about fees, please see the Resources at the end of this book.)

Multiple Plans

You can have several plans opened by several people (say the parents, grandparents, or an uncle) but, as with the other tax shelters, each plan must follow the maximum contribution rules. There is a lifetime contribution limit of $50,000 per beneficiary. If you had the funds, you could contribute the full amount in one year but you would miss out on getting the most from the government grant (see next section). You can contribute for beneficiaries who are under 31 years of age and the plan can remain open for a maximum of 35 years if beneficiaries want to postpone their post-secondary education.

Canada Education Savings Grant

The most attractive feature of the RESP is the Canada Education Savings Grant (CESG). For eligible beneficiaries under the age of 18, the government matches 20% of the first $2,500 contributed annually up to a maximum of $7,200 per beneficiary. Depending on your family income, the beneficiary could be eligible for an additional grant of up to 20% on the first $500 contributed towards the RESP per year.

Canada Learning Bond

If your child was born after 2003, you could receive the Canada Learning Bond. This is a $500 deposit from the federal government to jump-start your RESP. The child will also receive $100 per year until they reach 15.

Invested funds grow tax deferred as with the other shelters. When the beneficiary starts withdrawing funds, the dollars are taxed in their hands. Because beneficiaries will be in school full time, they will likely have little to no income and so would pay little to no tax on the funds received.

For more on RESPs and to learn more about provincial government incentives, see the **Resources** chapter.

TFSAs

The Tax-Free Savings Account (TFSA) was introduced in January 2009 and has been a huge hit with Canadians ever since. This account seems to create the most confusion because it's a fairly new shelter in Canada, but also I think calling it an "account" confuses the public as it is a tax shelter much like an RRSP or a RRIF.

TFSA Highlights

- $5,000 maximum annual contribution in after-tax dollars
- no tax deduction for your contribution
- any unused contribution room carried forward (starting from 2009)
- interest, dividends and capital gains are tax free (this is the first time we've ever been able to truly say "tax free" with any of the tax shelters)
- withdrawals are tax free.

Contributions in After-Tax Dollars

Any Canadian resident over 18 can contribute up to $5,000 per year to a TFSA. As with the RESP, but unlike the RRSP, the contribution is not tax deductible. In other words, the contribution cannot be deducted from your total income. You can invest in the same wide range of investments as for an RRSP. Any income or capital gains earned on the investments held in the TFSA are tax free and withdrawals are tax free. Where people have gotten into trouble is by withdrawing money and then redepositing it in the TFSA in the same year; withdrawals can be redeposited only in future years. Any unused contribution room can be carried forward indefinitely from the base year 2009. If you open a TFSA in 2012, for example, your total contribution limit is $20,000. The TFSA can be transferred to a spouse or common-law partner at the death of the account holder.

TFSA or RRSP?

Which is more effective as a tax shelter, the RRSP with its tax-deductible contribution or the TFSA with its tax-free withdrawals? This is difficult to answer. Each was designed for a different purpose and there is no single strategy for either tax shelter. Each has its advantages and disadvantages for people in different tax brackets and for people who need money for different purposes.

Advantages of RRSPs

The RRSP was designed to create a retirement fund to grow untouched over 20, 30 or more years. The government wants you to look after yourself by creating your own retirement fund and not rely solely on government pensions. Contribution levels are higher than those for a TFSA and withdrawals are discouraged by taxation. The government wants you to put a lot of money into your RRSP and keep it there, so many types of investments are sanctioned so that they can be sheltered in order to provide you with the maximum opportunity to make the most of opportunities to create capital gains and income.

Advantages of TFSAs

An RRSP is primarily intended for retirement, but a TFSA is like a savings plan for everything else in your life, because it can be used to save for any purpose, such as to purchase a new car, renovate a house, start a small business or take a family vacation. Your TFSA withdrawals and investment growth within your account are not included in your income—they are tax free. Also, if you withdraw money from your TFSA, the full amount being withdrawn can be put back into the TFSA in future years. You can also use the assets in a TFSA as collateral for a loan, something you cannot do with the assets in an RRSP.

RDSPs

The Registered Disability Savings Plan (RDSP) was introduced in 2008 and is the least understood and one of the most complex tax shelters in Canada. If you qualify for the Disability Tax Credit (or know someone that does), this savings plan could assist in strengthening your long-term financial security.

The government wants to making saving easier and offers a number of attractive enticements with the RDSP.

As with the other tax shelters, what you invest grows tax deferred (you're not taxed on it until you take the funds out). But with the RDSP, the government offers a grant and bond to qualifying beneficiaries. Even if you don't have the extra dollars to contribute to an RDSP, you can possibly benefit from the Canadian Disability Savings Grant (CDSG) and the Canadian Disability Savings Bond (CDSB):

- the CDSG provides matching grants up to 300% (it depends on the beneficiary's family income) and the amount contributed. The maximum is $3,500 per year and $70,000 over the beneficiary's lifetime.
- the CDSB is paid to lower-income Canadians with disabilities who qualify for payments to a RDSP up to a lifetime maximum of $20,000 (there's a $1,000 annual maximum). If you qualify, the government deposits the funds to your RDSP; however, you can receive the bond without contributing it to an RDSP.

RDSP Highlights

- the plan is set up in the name of the person with the disability
- beneficiary must be a Canadian resident under the age of 60 and eligible for the Disability Tax Credit
- long-term savings with no annual contribution limit
- broad choice of investment options (as with the other shelters above)
- once you set up a RDSP, you can then apply for the grant and bond
- there are multiple options when withdrawing funds, but withdrawals in excess of contributions are taxable and subject to complex rules
- annual payments must start by age 60 to the plan holder and there are options for one-time withdrawals as well (see the **Resources** chapter for more information)
- funds in your plan from the CDSG and CDSB must remain in there for at least 10 years
- no annual limit on contributions as long as the $200,000 lifetime contribution limit is not exceeded
- as of January 2011, you are allowed to claim unused CDSG and CDSB entitlements from the past 10 years (but you have to apply before age 49).

See the **Resources** section at the end of this book for provincial and territory benefits that you may also consider and for a list of participating financial organizations.

A Lot Can Be Done in Only 20 Years

This case shows how a RRIF and TFSA can work together to provide a pension fund. Note the effect of the higher withdrawals on the declining balance of the RRIF and the impact on tax rates.

Alexis has just turned 45 and the thought of retirement is starting to worry her. She got herself into trouble with debt in her late 30s when a business partner stole funds from her cupcake shop and left Alexis with large debts. She had to close the store and get a job in order to repay the loans. After a struggle, she paid off all her credit cards and other debt and is now renting an apartment in Vancouver.

Alexis has no investments and is wondering if she should contribute to an RRSP, TFSA or both. Her employer has no employee pension plan, but Alexis is not sure whether she'll even stay there for the rest of her working life. She currently earns $87,000 a year, so she could contribute $15,660 (18% of $87,000) to an RRSP annually. Since she no longer has huge monthly debt repayments, Alexis can easily allocate the $1,305 a month to her RRSP.

Assumptions:

- Alexis contributes $1,305 a month for the next 20 years until she's 65
- Her income remains the same for 20 years
- She has only interest-bearing securities in her portfolio that earn an average annual rate of return of 5% compounded
- Alexis redirects $5,000 of her annual $5,365 tax savings into a TFSA on which she also earns 5% per annum compounded

At age 65, when Alexis would like to retire, she will have $543,702 in an RRSP and $173,596 in a TFSA. Her savings over 20 years will provide a net worth (before taxes) of $701,749.

...continued

If Alexis retires at 65 and converts her RRSP to a RRIF, she will have to withdraw a minimum of 4.17% or $22,836 from her RRIF during the year in which she turns 66. If, at that time, she were to pay the present 20.06% marginal tax rate as a resident of British Columbia, she would pay $4,332 in taxes and have $17,261 left for her own use.

Given the history of her family, Alexis figures she could reasonably expect to live another 20 years after retirement. In that case, she could withdraw $8,267 annually from her TFSA and not attract tax while making her taxable RRSP withdrawals according to the schedule established by the CRA. When the percentage withdrawn exceeds her 5% growth rate on the investments that remain in the fund, she will be withdrawing an increasing portion of her declining balance. If, however, she is able to continue getting a 5% annual rate of return, the fund will last Alexis for the rest of her life.

The Garages

Here is a quick recap of all main tax shelters in Canada:

RRSP—Registered Retirement Savings Plan

- Incentives are designed to save for your retirement
- Your investments grow tax deferred
- You get a tax deduction when you contribute
- Withdrawals are subject to tax, except for Lifelong Learning Plan and Home Buyers' Plan
- You can contribute 18% of your earned income (up to yearly maximums)
- Deadline is March 1st in order to claim a deduction for the previous tax year

RRIF—Registered Retirement Income Fund

- Seamless conversion from an RRSP when you're ready to start using your funds
- Deadline to convert your RRSP into a RRIF is December 31 in the year you turn 71
- You must take at least a minimum amount out of the plan each year as set out by the government based on your age and plan value
- Any amount you take out will be subject to tax
- You can't put in any new investments
- Your assets continue to grow tax deferred

RESP—Registered Education Savings Plan

- Designed to help parents save for their children's post-secondary needs
- The government will match 20% of what you put in up to a maximum of $7,200
- You don't get a tax deduction, but the plan grows tax deferred
- The withdrawals are taxed in your child's hands, which are likely to be insignificant or nil
- You can set up family plans in case you're concerned one of your children might not choose higher learning
- There are options if one or none of your children choose to move on to post-secondary education

TFSA—Tax Free Savings Account

- You can contribute $5,000 a year
- Unused contribution room accumulates—e.g., could contribute $20,000 in 2012 if you hadn't contributed any funds since TFSAs started in 2009
- Your money grows tax free!
- You don't get a tax deduction
- You can invest in all sorts of assets just like the other tax shelters (not just bank accounts as many advertisers make us believe)
- You can take your money out any time (there might be rules, penalties and fees on the investments you sell, but no tax issue as with the other shelters)

RDSP—Registered Disability Savings Plan

- Designed to help those with severe disabilities save for their retirement
- Must be eligible for the Disability Tax Credit
- There is no annual maximum for contributions
- Proceeds of the plan grow tax deferred
- Depending on your income, may be eligible for the Canadian Disability Savings Grant and or the Canadian Disability Savings Bond
- Withdrawals are taxable and the plan must start paying out to the plan holder by the age of 60

Easy Action Steps

1. Go to your financial institution's website or call up your financial planner to see if an RRSP, TFSA or both are right for you.

2. Start your child's RESP as early as possible to take advantage of the government grant—it's like getting a guaranteed 20% return (up to the annual and lifetime maximum). Just remember to keep a balance of saving for your own retirement, reducing debt and maintaining a healthy emergency account.

3. Make sure your RRSP is working for you. The RRSP deadline can be hectic and to get your contribution in on time, your financial advisor may have just deposited it in a tax shelter paying little to no interest. A month or two after the deadline is a good time to review your portfolio and ensure you're diversified.

CHAPTER 10

IT'S NEVER TOO LATE TO START BEING MONEY SMART!

It's Never Too Late to Start Being Money Smart!

Taking care of your finances is a lot like getting in shape. It's easy to overeat and put on weight, just like it's easy to overspend and rack up debt. You can get physically fit if you change your habits and eat less and exercise more. Doing a little bit at a time and doing it regularly can do a lot for your fitness.

Being financially healthy requires the same discipline. You can get financially healthy if you change your habits and spend less and save/invest more and reduce your debt. It takes hard work, discipline and tough choices, but it can be done and it's never too late to start.

A recent survey for the CICA found that Canadians are saving less, spending more and taking on too much debt. If this describes your financial habits, it doesn't mean that you can't change. Having read this Guide, you know that being money smart is within the reach of everyone who is willing to learn and wants to take control of their present and future finances.

The ideal moment to start your financial plan is **right now!** Seize the day and take control. You have the means in your hands today to take action for yourself. The following are three important areas you should focus on first.

1. Start by Saving More

Pay Yourself First

The CICA survey found that 60% of Canadians save less than 10% of their monthly income and a third of these people save less than 5% or nothing at all.

You really need to save before you spend! Do not look upon savings as something left over after you've spent everything else. Save first, then live and budget with the net amount. As of January 2012, Statistics Canada reported that Canadians had an average annual salary of about $46,000. If we suppose that is the average salary for 40 years of working life, $1,840,000 will pass through your hands. If you saved just 10% over your lifetime—not even allowing for investment growth—you'd have $184,000 by just skimming a little off the top. Plus, with some investment acumen, that number would be significantly higher.

2. Start Spending Less

Put Yourself on the "30-Day Budget Diet"

Focus your fiscal thinking on how to make the most of the money available to you. Tracking your spending will reveal how much of your income is spent on wants rather than needs. Just as we thoughtlessly consume empty calories by continuing to eat even when we're not really hungry, we can carelessly create financial waste. You might be surprised at how much.

To manage your money better, you'll need to start by counting your financial calories on the 30-Day Budget Diet (see **chapter 2**):

Step 1: Track your spending for 30 days
Step 2: Categorize your spending
Step 3: Crunch the numbers
Step 4: Trim the fat.

3. Start Managing Your Cash, Credit Cards and Other Debt

Canadians are carrying more debt than ever before and nearly 50% of them would be challenged to keep up with mortgage or debt payments following a significant rise in interest rates. The use of credit card financing, often with double-digit interest rates, is on the rise. In 2012, 43% of Canadians reported carrying a balance on their credit cards, which is up significantly from 34% which was reported in 2010.

It has been said that if you want to curtail your spending, use cash, because paying with plastic happens so quickly you don't feel any loss. However, it's very difficult to get around in today's world without a credit card—the goal is to minimize carrying a balance. So, become aware of the benefits (and dangers) of credit cards and ensure you always make your payments on time!

Try to Say "No" to More Debt!

Almost 20% of Canadians have borrowed to cover day-to-day living expenses, and nearly half still owe against these loans. If the only way you can afford things you want (not need)—such as a vacation or new clothes or a new TV—is to charge it on a credit card/line of credit/no-payment-no-interest offer without a means of paying for it in the near future, save up for it instead, you'll enjoy your purchase much more and reduce your stress in the long-term.

Try to resist the temptation to take on more debt as no borrowed money is "free", it always has to be repaid.

Jane was depressed; she was in her late forties and newly divorced. For the first time in her life she was on her own. She was also in a really bad financial situation—she had no assets as her divorce had followed the loss of a family business (caused by a prolonged economic downturn) and all their family assets had been sold to pay off both their business and personal debts. Her credit score was at an all-time low.

She found a steady job with some benefits and a pension plan, but was very worried about her future—starting again with no credit and no assets—so she sought the advice of a financial advisor at her bank. The financial advisor suggested she could start her recovery by being careful with her spending and to take out a small RRSP loan to help her re-establish her credit while starting to save again for her retirement. The majority of the loan would be paid off by her tax rebate and she could afford to repay the remaining amount monthly over the following year.

Jane carefully assessed all her expenditures, used only cash for several years (when her improved credit score enabled her to get a credit card, she made sure to pay the balance off monthly), started to save a small amount each month and continued to get an RRSP loan and repay it promptly to help her credit score.

...continued

Within a few years, Jane had saved a minimal down payment and was able to get a mortgage (with her good credit score) and bought a condo. Her mortgage and fees were no more than her rent had been. Whenever she could she added to her RRSP and used her tax rebate to pay down her mortgage.

By the time Jane reached 65, she could look forward to her retirement with confidence—her mortgage was almost paid off, she received a company pension (as well as CPP and OAS) and she had a healthy amount in her RRSP.

Ready, Set, Go!

I hope that this Guide will help you start to make improvements in your financial health and you will make it a life-long goal to continue to do this. Keep this Guide handy and refer to it as your financial needs evolve. Be sure to visit **www.financialdecisionsmatter.com** for information, tips, resources and bonus material.

Here's to your financial success!

Resources

Go to CICA's **www.financialdecisionsmatter.com**

Generally

Financial Consumer Agency of Canada

This Government of Canada site provides information about banking, budgeting, credit cards, mortgages, insurance and credit. It also includes a tool to help you select a credit card, a calculator for your budget and consumer alerts.
www.fcac-acfc.gc.ca

Get Smarter About Money

This site was created by the Ontario Securities Commission's Investor Education Fund and provides "straight answers to money questions":
www.getsmarteraboutmoney.ca

RateSupermarket.ca

Helps you find the best rates on mortgages, credit cards, investing, life insurance, savings and bank accounts:
www.ratesupermarket.ca

Chapter 2

See **www.financialdecisionsmatter.com** for an Excel file of the Categorize Your Spending Worksheet.

Money Management Apps

Go to **www.appadvice.com** to read reviews on many different financial apps. Sign up for their Apps Gone Free program to get notified of any paid apps that have a special limited time promotion.

Chapter 3

See **www.financialdecisionsmatter.com** for Excel files:

- Permanent record checklist
- Personal Information Checklist
- Records checklist
- Sample monthly payments checklist

Virtual Shoebox

The Canadian Life and Health Insurance association have created a "virtual shoebox" tool to help you keep track of your personal records:

Go to **www.clhia.ca**, click on **For Consumers** and then click on **Virtual Shoebox**

Chapter 4

Talking with Your Kids

A Parent's Guide to Raising Money-Smart Kids
For more information and to purchase an eBook or print copy, go to
CAstore.ca/moneysmartkids

Talking with Your Parents

See *A Guide to Financial Decisions: Planning for the End of Life*. To download a free eBook or PDF, go to
www.financialdecisionsmatter.com

Talking with Financial Professionals

Financial Planners
For the Six-Step Financial Planning Process, go to
www.cifps.ca/CifpsAdmin/Media/PDF/TheSixStepProcessToFinancialPlanning.pdf
How do I find a financial planner?
To find a planner in good standing, go to the Financial Planning Standards Council (FPSC) website at
www.fpsc.ca/directory-cfp-professionals-good-standing

Life Insurance Agent
It is advisable to use an advisor who is a member of a professional association.
Advocis: The Financial Advisors Association of Canada
www.advocis.ca/forpublic.html
Canadian Life and Health Insurance Association (CLHIA)
www.clhia.ca

Your InsuranceBrokers.com

This is a consumer-orientated resource indexing licensed life insurance brokers across Canada who represent more than one insurance company and who demonstrate their ability to "shop" on behalf of the consumer. The site has many useful consumer resources:

www.yourinsurancebroker.com

Disputes

If you need help with a complaint, try the following websites:

- your local Better Business Bureau: **www.bbb.org**
- if it's against a bank or trust company, the Ombudsman: **www.obsi.ca**
- if it's your life and health insurance company or insurance coverage, contact the OmbudService for Life and Health Insurance (OLHI) for bilingual information and assistance: **www.olhi.ca**
- if it's in general, the Office of Consumer Affairs: **www.ic.gc.ca/eic/site/oca-bc.nsf/eng/h_ca02207.html**

The Government of Canada also has a website that details to whom you should direct your complaints, but also the rights you have as a consumer in the area of banking, mortgages, credit and much more:

www.fcac-acfc.gc.ca/eng/consumers/rights/index-eng.asp

Chapter 5

Canadian Home Ownership

See the May 2012 report *Confidence in the Canadian Mortgage Market* published by the Canadian Association of Accredited Mortgage Professionals (CAAMP): **caamp.org/meloncms/media/Spring%20report%202012_ENG.pdf**

Preparing to Buy

If you are preparing to buy a house or condominium, the best place to start is the Canada Mortgage and Housing Corporation (CMHC) website:

www.cmhc.ca/en/index.cfm

Mortgage Rates

To search rates by city, by bank, by type of mortgage and also to look for a mortgage broker:

www.ratehub.ca

Chapter 7

Credit Report

To obtain a copy of your credit report:

- Equifax Canada **www.equifax.ca**
- TransUnion Canada **www.transunion.ca**

Note: Be sure to use ".ca" and not ".com" for the Canadian sites.

Protect Yourself Against Identity Theft

For a Consumer Identity Theft Checklist from the Government of Canada:
http://cmcweb.ic.gc.ca/eic/site/cmc-cmc.nsf/eng/fe00088.html

For suggestions from the Privacy Commissioner of Canada:
www.priv.gc.ca/resource/fs-fi/id/primer_e.asp

"Nine Things You Absolutely Must Do to Keep Your Online Identity Secure"
http://gizmodo.com/5932663/9-things-you-absolutely-must-do-to-keep-your-online-identity-secure

The Identity Theft and Identity Fraud Victim Assistance Guide
www.antifraudcentre-centreantifraude.ca/english/documents/victimguide.pdf

Victim of Identity Theft

For information on how to act fast if you think you've been a victim of fraud, see the RCMP site:
www.rcmp-grc.gc.ca/scams-fraudes/victims-guide-victimes-eng.htm

If you suspect a scam:

- contact the Canadian Anti-Fraud Centre (1-888-495-8501) or your local police.
- place a Fraud Alert on your file with each of the two Canadian Credit agencies
  - Equifax (1-866-828-5961)
  - TransUnion (1-800-663-9980)

The **Canadian Anti-Fraud Centre** is a joint operation between the Royal Canadian Mounted Police, the Ontario Provincial Police and the Competition Bureau Canada to create a national fraud reporting centre for victims and complainants of all fraud types:
www.antifraudcentre.ca

Credit Counselling
For more information and to find a professional credit counsellor:
www.caccs.ca/agencies.html
www.creditcanada.com

Chapter 8

"Investing 101"
The Investor Education Fund's Get Smarter About Money website can help you get started:
www.getsmarteraboutmoney.ca/en/managing-your-money/investing/Pages/default.aspx

CDIC

Make sure your financial institution is a CDIC member or insured under a provincial plan
For a complete list of members, visit the CDIC website at **www.cdic.ca** and click on "Where Are My Savings Insured by CDIC". Only deposits at member institutions are insured.

Chapter 9

RESP
www.hrsdc.gc.ca/eng/learning/education_savings/public/resp.shtml

Fees
www.getsmarteraboutmoney.ca/en/managing-your-money/investing/resps-for-education/Pages/resp-fees.aspx

Education Savings Incentives
www.hrsdc.gc.ca/eng/learning/education_savings/publications_resources/promoter/tools/guide/1-1-1.shtml

Canada Education Savings Grant
www.hrsdc.gc.ca/eng/learning/education_savings/public/cesg.shtml

Canada Learning Bond
www.hrsdc.gc.ca/eng/learning/education_savings/public/clb.shtml

Using Your RESP
www.canlearn.ca/eng/saving/resp/program.shtml

TFSA
www.tfsa.gc.ca/

Also go to the website of your bank/financial institution.

RDSP
For information on annual payments to the plan holder and one-time withdrawals:
www.cra-arc.gc.ca/tx/ndvdls/tpcs/rdsp-reei/pmnts/typsmd-eng.html

There are provincial and territory benefits that you may consider as well:
www.hrsdc.gc.ca/eng/disability_issues/disability_savings/rdsp_ptb.shtml

For a list of participating financial organizations:
www.hrsdc.gc.ca/eng/disability_issues/disability_savings/financ_org.shtml

Acknowledgements

They say it takes a village to raise a child. Well, it certainly does to produce a book and (wrongfully) the author gets all the credit.

I'm incredibly grateful to the professional team at CICA: Cairine Wilson, Vice-President, Member Services, for initiating and believing in this project every step of the way and also to Nicholas Cheung, Director, Program and Publication Development, for his dedication, passion and keen eye as a CA and advocate of financial literacy; they both brought great enthusiasm to this project which will serve Canadians well.

My deepest thanks to Maggie Tyson, Manager, Editorial Development, who co-ordinated this entire project and was a godsend; she's the kind of editor that every writer dreams about working with. I'd also like to thank Michael Dave Dizon, Art Director, for his creative design, Susan Smith for her keen eye in quality control and Li Zhang, Program Manager, Financial Literacy. This book also benefits from the extremely helpful research and editing of Doug Adamson.

A very special thanks to all that offered advice, insight, interviews and more: John Haliburton from SunLife Financial, Joyce Yamashita and Laura MacKenzie from the York Region District School Board, Scott Hutchinson from the Privacy Commissioner's Office, Keith Costello from the CIFPS, Kristin Doucet and Greg Pollock from Advocis, Laurie Campbell from Credit Canada Debt Solutions, Yolanda Van Wachem from McLennan Ross, Sarah Hanson and Cesar Rainusso from BMO InvestorLine.

Special thanks to my patient and brilliant husband for being an inspiration and sounding board through every stage of this project (and for allowing me to drive him crazy some days!) and for encouraging me to share my ideas as an author before I ever realized I could. Also to my incredible mother, Kathleen, and my amazing family, Randy, David, Elaine, Amelia, Alysha, Marc, Jocelyn and Adam, for all their love and support, plus thanks to a few furry friends at home!

Finally, this and every book I have written wouldn't be possible without the strength of my Creator, God, for giving me the energy to complete another project to fulfill my passion of making Canadians feel good about money!

About the Author

Kelley Keehn is a personal finance expert, speaker, media personality and author of eight books including ***The Money Book for Everyone Else***, ***She Inc.***, ***The Woman's Guide to Money*** and ***The Prosperity Factor for Kids***.

During the decade she spent as a financial professional and the last seven years since leaving the industry, Kelley discovered that whether someone has a billion in the bank or is a million in the hole, everyone has money problems! While working in the banking and financial industry, she witnessed how emotions can reinforce the problems that individuals have with money. She has developed a number of fun and practical guides to uncover and change people's money mindsets at a fundamental level.

Kelley is a popular media guest, appearing on TV and radio around the globe, and has written many columns and published articles. She has been a regular contributor for CNBC (New York), a nationally syndicated columnist with CBC radio, the host of W Network's *Burn My Mortgage*, a weekly columnist for the *Globe and Mail*, and AOL's WalletPop Canada. She is a frequent guest on the *Marilyn Denis Show* and has been quoted in Oprah's *O Magazine*.

Kelley is thrilled that her newest book, ***A Canadian's Guide to Money-Smart Living*** is part of the CICA's literacy campaign, released in the fall/winter of 2012, which expands her mission for Canadians to *feel good about money*!

For more information, please visit **www.kelleykeehn.com**.